Everyman's Database Primer

featuring dBASE II

Published by
Ashton-Tate
10150 W. Jefferson Blvd.
Culver City, CA 90230
(213) 204-5570

By
Robert A. Byers

Virginia Bare, Editor

Cover by Peter Green

Book design and management of production
by Virginia Bare

Illustrations by
D. A. Gray

Copyright © 1982 by Ashton-Tate
10150 West Jefferson Boulevard
Culver City, California 90230
(213) 204-5570

ISBN 0-912677-00-7

dBASE II is a trademark of Ashton-Tate

Printed in the United States of America

First printing November, 1982

ACKNOWLEDGEMENT

I wish to thank all of those who have contributed in one way or another to this book. George Tate and Wayne Ratliff who suggested it in the first place and then provided encouragement and advice along the way. Virginia Bare who has patiently and skillfully edited the manuscript. My sons, Kenneth and Robert Jr. who cheerfully reviewed the early manuscript and offered support and encouragement. And finally, Charlene Ebert who was responsible for getting me interested in database management for micro-computers in the first place.

TABLE OF CONTENTS

Page

SECTION ONE

Section One introduces 'databases' and acquaints us with how they work. Databases are very common in our daily surroundings and we rarely think twice about their part in our routine functioning. A 'database management system' is simply the way these familiar databases are contained in and manipulated by a computer.

We will take a close look at some common database examples. This allows us to dissect the pieces of a database and understand how a database system works to provide us with organized information. The process is so simple: we will start right away, turn our computer on and make our first computer databases.

CHAPTER I

DATABASE

'Database' is computer jargon for a quite familiar and essential item in our everyday lives. A database is a collection of information organized and presented to serve a specific purpose.

One of the more familiar database examples is the Telephone Directory. This common printed database contains the names, addresses and telephone numbers of individuals, businesses, and government agencies. The addresses and telephone numbers have little value by themselves. They are useful only when they are RELATED to a name.

When we reflect upon it, the number of databases we are familiar with is really astonishing. Some of the more common databases are: a dictionary, a cookbook, a Sears-Roebuck Catalog, an encyclopedia, the card catalog at the library, your checkbook, etc. Other databases more or less familiar, depending on one's background are: the stockmarket report in the newspaper, an accounts receivable ledger, a personnel file etc.

Now, why do we consider these examples to be databases? Why isn't the newspaper, or a non-fiction book considered a database? After all, they do contain information. The reason is quite specific. In each of the examples given above, information is presented in a manner which makes it easy for the user to locate some particular piece of information of interest. In the telephone directory example, telephone numbers and addresses are related to the name. The names are presented in alphabetical order so one can find them easily. Find the name and you have found the phone number. The name is the KEY to using the phone book. The dictionary example is quite similar. There is a word and a definition. The words are listed alphabetically so that they can be found. The definition is related to the word. The KEY to use of the dictionary is the word.

Database

The common element in all of the examples is *organized information presented in a way that makes it easy to find* — by the use of some KEY. In other words, information that can be presented as tables (rows and columns) can be a database. Some examples of column headings in tables that could be considered databases are shown in Figure 1-1.

Examples:		Column Headings		
PHONE BOOK:	NAME	ADDRESS	PHONE NUMBER	
DICTIONARY:	WORD	DEFINITION		
CATALOG:	ITEM	DESCRIPTION	WEIGHT	SIZE
	COST		PART NO.	
STOCK REPORT:	STOCK	SHARES TRADED	HIGH	LOW

Figure 1-1. Examples of Column Headings From
Some Common Paper Databases

By now you should have a general concept of a database, and you might be asking: 'O.K., but what's a *computer* database? What can I do with it that I can't do without it?' The computer database can't do anything you couldn't do yourself from a printed database. However, some things possible without the computer are simply not practical. As an example, we have all found a scrap of paper with a phone number on it — no name, just a number. If we want to find out who the number belongs to, the telephone book isn't much help. If, however, the telephone directory is a computer database, we can ask the computer who belongs to the phone number and the name will promptly appear.

As another example, suppose you want the phone number of someone named Smith who lives on Santa Monica Blvd. in Los Angeles. You can ask the computer's L.A. phone book file (maybe named 'LAPHONE') for the names, addresses, and phone numbers of all of the Smiths on Santa Monica Blvd. It may not give you a single name and number, but it will surely narrow it down a lot.

The computer is no panacea. It can't do anything you can't. But — and it's a big but — it can *help* you do the things you want to do quickly and easily. It is a tool to help you accomplish things that are simply not practical without it.

Using a personal phone book as an example, a simple database might look something like the one shown in Figure 1-2.

NAME	ADDRESS	PHONE NUMBER
Byers, Robert A Sr	9999 Glencrest, Standale	555-9242
Byers, Robert A Jr	48 N. Catalina, Pasadena	555-9540
Cassidy, Butch	4800 Rimrock Ct., Sunland	878-1121
Evans, Sydney H.	398 S. Calif. Blvd., Encino	998-1234
Goose, Sil E.	21809 Cottage Ln., Montecito	675-1212
Hedman, Gene	139 Luxury Dr., Bev. Hills	987-6543
Maori, Stanislas	2800 Oak St. #344, Red. Bch.	324-8529
Robertson, James	5892 Glencrest, Standale	997-2741

Figure 1-2. A Sample Database

Of course, a real database might contain many, many more items of information. In fact, the above database is much better kept in a small notebook than in a computer. You can carry it around with you, make notes in it, and it's a lot cheaper. To get value from a computer you need a lot of information — in general, so much information that you can't efficiently use it without the computer. The purpose of this book is to teach you about databases and how to use them. Therefore, we are going to use very small databases for examples. Exactly the same principles would apply if this personal phone book was the White Pages for Los Angeles County. There is absolutely no difference other than a lot more entries in the white pages.

To better acquaint you with computer databases —

- how to plan them
- how to make them
- how to use them, and
- how to change them

we are going to build a computer database from a simple telephone book example. To do this, we will use the microcomputer database system 'dBASE II.' dBASE II is representative of the better database management systems currently available for microcomputers. A database management system is a system that can be installed on a computer, takes care of all of the details involved with a database, and allows the user to use, manipulate, and change the database contents.

If you own or have access to a microcomputer with dBASE II, you can follow the instructions in this book and work along using your computer. If you do not have either a microcomputer or dBASE II you will still be able to follow along without difficulty. A description of what you do, and what the computer does, will be provided at each step. What the computer 'does' will appear on the screen illustrations in regular type; what you 'do' — what you TYPE IN — will appear in BOLD type.

FROM PERSONAL PHONE BOOK TO COMPUTER DATABASE: THE QUESTION OF TERMINOLOGY

Let's look again at the data from our personal phone book.

THE RECORD

Byers, Robert A Sr   9999 Glencrest, Standale   555-9242

The entry as shown above is called a RECORD. Pieces of information that make up a RECORD are seen horizontally — displayed in rows across the page on screen. Our phone book has eight rows — eight RECORDS — eight sets of name + address + phone number.

THE FIELD

If we were to draw lines between the names and addresses and the addresses and phone numbers in our telephone book,

we would isolate columns of similar information. We would separate 3 groups of vertically arranged data — a column of names, a column of addresses and a column of phone numbers. In computer terminology, these columns are called FIELDS.

So, the example above, then, has EIGHT records and THREE fields.

FIELDNAMES

The column titles, NAME, ADDRESS, and PHONE NUMBER, are called FIELDNAMES. That's one word — FIELDNAME.

Conceptually, a computer database is the same as one that you could create with paper and a pencil. Obviously, both a paper database and a computer database exist to be USED. So, an appropriate question is: what do you actually DO with your phone book?

You write in new acquaintances, perhaps change names, addresses or phone numbers of people who move, get a new phone, marry or divorce. Maybe you cross some people out (or erase them, if you've been so foresighted to keep your records in pencil. . .). When you want to use the information stored there, likely you are trying to make a call, going to a party at a particular address, mailing a letter.

Your phone book — if you keep it up to date — reflects a process of change and, at any given time, will supply you with information you're looking for. The same is true of your computer database.

You can very easily add, take out or change the information in a computer database. Likewise, you can get information from your computer database to look at — and do so very easily.

In your everyday activities, you are always adding and subtracting from information at hand, changing it, picking out what you want to see and ignoring what you don't want to see. This activity is the basic process of our intelligence — the process is really very familiar.

But, we are talking about putting all this information we're so accustomed to having strewn all around us in a 'computer database.' There will be something holding this information — between us and it, so to speak. We need to become comfortable with the fact that it's in there. We need to know that we can get the information out when we need to use it. After we become comfortable, then we can be amazed at how much a computer database can actually do for our information needs.

Using your computer will become as easy as using your phone book. Like anything you do in life, it takes some thought, some planning and some 'how-to' knowledge. You need to know how to create, how to use and how to change your store of information. In the learning process, it will not be necessary for you to comprehend how to reinvent the wheel. You are only learning a new function — a new set of mechanics for a new machine — designed to support your efforts to perceive and process all kinds of information already very familiar to you.

So, we will introduce you to computer databases. Together we will build and use some simple ones. So that you can easily relate the principles and common examples to actual practice, we will use dBASE II, a commercial microcomputer database management system. dBASE II is representative of database management systems currently available for microcomputers.

SOME SIMPLE ANALOGIES

Let's look at another simple example to illustrate the concept behind a database management system. Say you need a part for your car. You go to an auto parts store and tell the clerk which part you want. He looks up the part in a set of parts catalogs.

- The first book gives him an identifying number for the part.

- He then looks up this part number in another book. This book tells him where the part is located within the store.

- After he gets the part he again uses the number to find the cost of the part from a price list.

In this analogy, the actual automotive parts correspond to the data items in the database. The clerk, catalogs, lists, storage bins, etc. correspond to the database management system. To use this 'automotive parts management system' you tell the clerk what you want in a language that he understands (English) using terminology related to cars. 'I need a carburetor for a 76 Belchfire 8.' The clerk takes care of all of the business of getting the parts, keeping the books current, knowing how to use the books, etc. All you need to do is have a reasonable idea of what you want. The clerk and his books and catalogs take care of the rest.

The same is true for the computer database management system (DBMS). As soon as a DBMS is 'installed' on a computer, the computer becomes an 'expert' at all of the details involved in storing, cataloging, and retrieving data. All you need to do is have a reasonable idea of what you want and know a little computer terminology. This book provides you with the computer terminology you need. The computer and the database management system take care of the rest.

Incidentally, don't be frightened by the need to 'install' the database management system on the computer. It's nothing like the 'ready-to-assemble' toys children often get as presents. It's simple.

Another analogy to a database management system is apparent in a large library. In many large libraries, particularly university research libraries, one is not ordinarily allowed access to the shelves where the books are stored. To acquire a book you must consult the card catalog, copy information from the index card to a slip of paper, and hand the paper to a librarian.

Then — unseen by you a 'gnome' will scuttle through dark passageways to retrieve the book and deliver it to the librarian to deliver to you.

When you return the book, much of this process is reversed. The librarian gives the book to a 'gnome' who scuttles back to place the book in the location that it originally occupied. Again, the card catalog, the librarian, the 'gnomes', and the storage facilities correspond to the computer database management system. The book corresponds to the data item. All that is required of you is a little knowledge of how to use this system. The system does all the work.

OUR FIRST COMPUTER DATABASE

We have talked at length about our personal phone book. It is a good basis for making our first computer database. We will use it as an example and, as we proceed, you'll see that the process isn't much different from putting the information on a sheet of paper with an ordinary typewriter.

Say we were going to type this information on a piece of paper. Typically, whichever one of us has agreed to do the typing might do three things:

(1) enter column headings such as Name, Address, and Phone Number;

(2) figure out how many spaces to use for each column to keep everything neat and orderly; and

(3) type in a page heading or title for the page.

In a computer database, these activities are not optional.

- You must assign FIELDNAMES for each column (FIELD).

- You must figure out the size of each column — this is called the FIELD WIDTH.

- And, you must give the database a title. The database title is called a FILENAME.

We are almost ready to start making our computerized version of a personal phone book. But before we go any farther you should know that computers have strange limitations.

If you were to take a pencil and paper and make a list of your friends' names, addresses and telephone numbers you might give the list a title, such as 'phone book', 'telephone list', etc. Before you can get the computer to accept a list you *must* give it a title. This title will be the name of the database.

Generally, a database is called a file and the title is called a FILENAME. FILENAMES have certain peculiarities.

- They cannot have more than EIGHT letters and numbers.
- They cannot contain any 'unused' or blank spaces.
- They must start with a LETTER.

In addition, the FILENAME is normally preceeded by an additional symbol. This identifies to the computer which disk drive is to be used for the data file. A disk drive is a device that is commonly used to store information. Computer storage devices such as disk drives will be more fully explained in Chapter 3.

There is often more than one such disk drive attached to the computer. The disk identifier is the method for informing the computer which device is to be used. In this text the disk drives are identified by a letter followed by a colon — such as 'A:'. This is a convention which is used by many microcomputer systems.

Some possible titles (FILENAMES) for our computerized telephone book (database) are shown in Figure 1-3. Please bear in mind that you can give the database any name with 8 or fewer letters.

```
                              A:TELEFONE
        (for disk drive A)    A:FONEBOOK
                              A:FONELIST


               OR


                              B:TELEFONE
        (for disk drive B)    B:FONEBOOK
                              B:FONELIST

        Figure 1-3. Sample Database Names
```

The filenames shown in the above example are called mnemonics. A mnemonic isn't a real word, but a group of letters whose phonetic pronunciation provides a clue to its meaning. It is usually a good idea to choose filenames in this manner. The following five 'words' are examples of mnemonics eligible to be file names.

ACCTSPAY   ACCTSREC   PAYROLL   PERSONNL   QTRLYTAX

FIELDNAME

Column headings (FIELDNAMES) must be assigned to each of the columns (FIELDS) in the database. FIELDNAMES have limitations similar to those for FILENAMES.

- They cannot have more than TEN letters and numbers.
- They cannot contain spaces.
- They must begin with a LETTER.

13

Our simple phone list has three column headings (FIELDNAMES); NAME, ADDRESS, and PHONE NUMBER. The first two (NAME,ADDRESS) are usable as FIELDNAMES, but PHONE NUMBER is not. It has more than 10 letters and contains a space which is not a letter or a number. So, we have to name this column with a mneumonic something like FONENUMBER or PHONE or NUMBER to conform to the 10 character rule.

FIELDTYPE

It is also necessary to tell the computer how many characters, (letters, numbers, spaces and other symbols) will be needed for each FIELD. You will enter a number equal to the total 'slots' necessary to hold the characters, spaces and other symbols.

Since the computer deals differently with different kinds of fields, it will need to know which of the three available fields is appropriate to our needs. Fields can be one of three kinds:

CHARACTER,

NUMERIC, or

LOGICAL.

In our example, all the FIELDS are CHARACTER FIELDS and may contain letters, numbers, spaces and other standard typewriter symbols. NUMERIC and LOGICAL FIELDS will be explained fully in later examples.

The computer does some things on its own. Each time a record is entered the computer automatically gives it a number. It calls the first row, which is the first record, RECORD 1, the second RECORD 2 and so forth. This is sort of interesting, but you might say, so what? You could, indeed, work with databases for a long time and do some very involved work without ever using a record number. They are, however, convenient for some things and we will discuss their usefulness later in this book.

We have covered, then, some basic, pertinent terminology. Make sure you are comfortable with the concepts because we are next going to construct a simple database. Remember:

Rows are Records, automatically numbered by the computer.

Columns are Fields: they need titles called FIELDNAMES (10 characters maximum, no spaces, start with a letter)

You must give your database a title, in other words a FILENAME (8 characters maximum, no spaces, start with letter)

You must tell the computer where (which disk drive) to put the data (Example: A:FONEBOOK will put it on 'A' drive)

Tell the computer the form and arrangement of information to be entered. You know about FILENAME & FIELDNAMES. Finish the task by (1) allocating the number of spaces necessary to accommodate information for each field, and (2) telling the computer whether the field is character, numeric or logical.

OUR FIRST EXERCISE

In this first exercise we will really start from scratch. When the computer is first turned on, the video screen will display something similar to Screen 1-1.

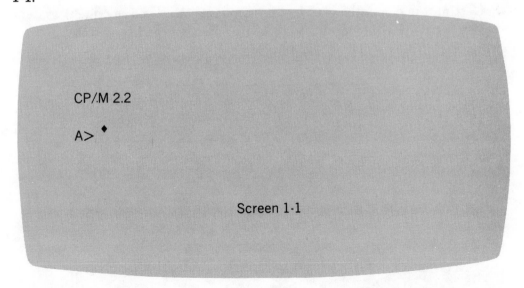

CP/M 2.2

A>

Screen 1-1

THE OPERATING SYSTEM

*CP/M® 2.2 is a widely used 'operating system' for microcomputers. An operating system helps you to operate the computer. CP/M® stands for Control Program for Microcomputers. Commercially available database management systems such as dBASE II use the operating system to perform routine tasks. You will not need to learn the details of the operating system to use a database management system.

The operating system sometimes imposes specific ways of doing things on the database system. For all of the examples in this book we will use CP/M® operating system conventions. CP/M® is a product of Digital Research of Pacific Grove, California. The number 2.2 is the version number. A version number is similar to a model number.

*CP/M is a registered trademark of Digital Research, Inc.

The A> is a PROMPT. It is the operating system's way of telling you 'I'm ready. Tell me what to do.' The symbol to the right of the > is called the cursor. The cursor is a light marker which appears on the screen to show you where you are. It is the computer's equivalent of a pencil point. Letters you 'type' on the screen by pressing keys on the keyboard will appear where the cursor is. As each letter is typed the cursor moves to the right.

GETTING YOUR COMPUTER TO USE dBASE II

Getting the computer ready to use your database management system is called LOADING the database. To begin, simply type in the letters DBASE. The video display will now look like Screen 1-2.

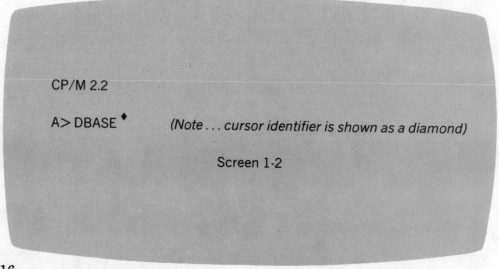

```
CP/M 2.2

A> DBASE ◆        (Note . . . cursor identifier is shown as a diamond)


              Screen 1-2
```

Press the RETURN key. The RETURN key is sort of interesting. The name is borrowed from the carriage return on an electric typewriter. For computer operation the key should probably be labeled ENTRY or ACCEPT or some such term. For most computer operations it indicates to the computer 'O.K. That's it, I'm through entering this item — now do it.'

The computer will respond as shown in Screen 1-3.

```
CP/M 2.2

A> DBASE

PLEASE ENTER TODAY'S DATE MM/DD/YY OR PRESS RETURN: ♦


                        Screen 1-3
```

The cursor is positioned for you to enter the date as requested. Enter the date as requested. The video display will now appear as illustrated in Screen 1-4. Note that the display began at the top of the screen and has progressed downward.

```
CP/M 2.2

A> DBASE

PLEASE ENTER TODAY'S DATE MM/DD/YY OR PRESS RETURN:  3/1/82

*** DBASE II          VERSION 2.3          15 FEB 1982

    ♦

                        Screen 1-4
```

The period at the far left of the screen under the asterisks is important. In dBASE II it is called a DOT PROMPT. The DOT PROMPT is the computer's way of telling you 'I'm ready, tell me to do something.' The things that you will tell it to do are called COMMANDS.

To get out of dBASE II, you simply type the word QUIT after a dot prompt:

.QUIT

The computer will respond with.

END RUN DBASE II

A>

You are now back to your computer's operating system.

The line following the date request line tells you exactly what you have 'installed.' dBASE II is the name of the database management system, 'Version 2.3' tells you what 'edition' of dBASE II you are using and the date that follows is the release date of version 2.3. A version number is like a model identifier. Normally each new version will have all of the features of earlier versions, plus new and/or improved features.

We are ready to start the process of CREATING the database B:FONEBOOK. The dialog between the user and the computer is shown in Screen 1-5. The computer responses (PROMPTS) and the corresponding keyboard entries are shown as they might appear on a video terminal. The computer prompts are in regular type. The keyboard entries are in **bold faced heavy black type**. On an actual video screen the keyboard entries would appear at normal intensity while the computer prompts would appear at a reduced intensity. Note that what we have done so far remains on the screen as we proceed.....

```
CP/M 2.2

A> DBASE

PLEASE ENTER TODAY'S DATE MM/DD/YY OR PRESS RETURN:  3/1/82

*** DBASE II          VERSION 2.3          15 FEB 1982

.CREATE
ENTER FILENAME:  B:FONEBOOK
ENTER RECORD STRUCTURE AS FOLLOWS:
  FIELD           NAME,TYPE,WIDTH,DECIMALPLACES
  001             NAME,C,20
  002             ADDRESS,C,40
  003             PHONE,C,8
  004

INPUT DATA NOW? Y ♦
```

Screen 1-5

Now we will enter the information which defines to the computer the form and arrangement of the database.

Just after the DOT PROMPT, type in the word CREATE. Then press the RETURN key. CREATE is the dBASE II COMMAND that starts the process of building the database. RETURN tells the computer to accept the COMMAND that you have just typed in (CREATE). Remember, the computer will do nothing until you press RETURN.

After you have entered CREATE (and pressed the RETURN key), the computer will respond with the prompt ENTER FILENAME:. The proper keyboard entry is — disk drive identifier, colon, and the eight-letter (and number) filename. In our example, the keyboard entry is B:FONEBOOK.

The next computer prompt will ask you to enter the fieldname, the type of field, and the size of the field (how many characters there are). It displays.

```
ENTER RECORD STRUCTURE AS FOLLOWS:
FIELD            NAME,TYPE,WIDTH,DECIMALPLACES
001
```

Remember the fieldname may have up to ten letters and numbers starting with a LETTER. A fieldname may not contain a space.

The first field is a character field whose FIELDNAME is NAME. We might decide to use 20 characters for this field. The keyboard entry is **NAME,C,20**. Then press the RETURN key. Notice that the computer prompt also asked for decimal places. No keyboard entry was required (or given) because the field was a character field. For character fields we disregard the computer's request for decimal places. The capital C between the two commas tells the computer that this is a character field. Commas are required between fieldname,fieldtype,width, and decimal places (if any).

The computer also displayed a field number 001 as a part of the prompt. This is automatic like the computer's numbering of records. This means the information you will enter is the description of the first field.

When the return key is pressed, after **NAME, C, 20** the computer immediately responds with 002. This tells you it is now ready to accept the fieldname, the fieldtype, and the size of the second field. This process will continue until you have either entered thirty-two field descriptions (maximum for dBASE II) or terminated the process. Don't worry if you think you may· someday want more than 32 fieldnames — it is possible but more complex. You will learn later how to accommodate more than 32 fields if your database requires more.

The process may be terminated at any time by pressing the RETURN key instead of entering the field definition. In the example, the RETURN was pressed when the computer asked for the definition of field 004. That is because we are only using three fields in this database (NAME, ADDRESS, PHONE).

ENTERING DATA

The computer will now ask you if you want to input (enter) data now. You should respond with a Y for yes or an N for no. You won't need to press the RETURN key; the computer will respond directly to the Y or N in this case.

A yes response will cause the computer to clear the video screen and begin prompting you to enter the names, addresses, and phone numbers (data). Enter 'Y' and the video screen will appear to you as shown in Screen 1-6.

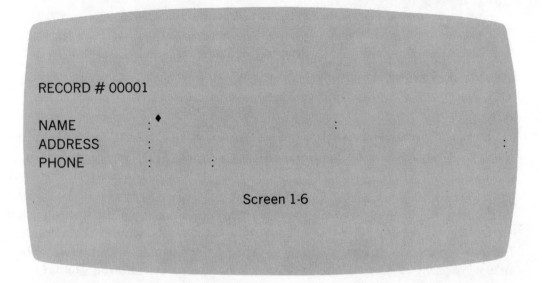

```
RECORD # 00001

NAME        :◆                        :
ADDRESS     :                                          :
PHONE       :          :


                    Screen 1-6
```

The display generated by the computer will appear at reduced intensity. The colons indicate the beginning and the end of the space allocated to the field whose fieldname appears to the left of the leftmost colon.

This kind of display is a full screen prompt. It prompts you to provide all information needed for the entire screen (as opposed to a dot prompt which asks for just one line of input). The computer displays the fieldnames and a space in which you are expected to enter the information belonging to the field (column).

As you enter the data for the name field, for example, the cursor will move to the right until the field is full. At this point, a bell will ring and the cursor will jump to the leftmost position of the next field. If, as is most likely, the name entered does not completely fill the space allocated to the name field you must press the RETURN key when the name has been completely entered. When you press the return key the cursor will move to the next field (in this case the ADDRESS field).

When you have entered all of the data for a record, as shown in Screen 1-7, the computer will automatically clear the screen and begin prompting you to enter data for the following record. This process is continued until you have entered all of the data.

```
RECORD # 00001

NAME            :BYERS, ROBERT A SR.        :
ADDRESS         :3481 GLENCREST, STANDALE        :
PHONE           :555-9242:

                        Screen 1-7
```

Earlier we had identified fields as *vertical* columns. Now the data for the vertical columns is entered as consecutive rows on the screen. This is done for convenience in entering the data. The computer places each field entry into a 'vertical column' in the database. When you have entered the data for the eight records of our example the screen will look like Screen 6 except the Record Number will read 0009, awaiting the ninth record. But we don't have a ninth this time.

If you press the return key now — with the cursor positioned as shown — the computer will exit from CREATE, and will respond with a DOT PROMPT, indicating that it is ready to accept further commands.

USING THE DATABASE

We now have a database. It has eight records and three fields; NAME,ADDRESS,PHONE. Its FILENAME (title) is FONEBOOK, and it is on the B drive. To use the database we type USE B:FONEBOOK (and a RETURN) after a DOT PROMPT.

.USE B:FONEBOOK

The computer responds with another DOT PROMPT on the next line. You may have many databases available on your computer. Via 'B:FONEBOOK' you tell the computer you want to work specifically with the database located on B:drive, whose FILENAME is FONEBOOK. USE is the dBASE II

22

COMMAND, roughly analogous to saying to your assistant, 'Chatsworth, please get me the phone book.' The transaction will look like this:

.USE B:FONEBOOK
♦

When the computer responds with the DOT PROMPT on the line just below USE B:FONEBOOK, the database FONEBOOK is ready for use.

Let's 'use' it first to look at the structure as we recently set it up. The structure of the database is really determined by the definition of the FIELDS (columns). To review the structure, type DISPLAY STRUCTURE following a DOT PROMPT. The computer will respond with the display shown in Screen 1-8.

```
. DISPLAY STRUCTURE                              (Keyboard Command)

STRUCTURE FOR FILE:     B:FONEBOOK.DBF
NUMBER OF RECORDS:     00008
DATE OF LAST UPDATE:  9/15/81
PRIMARY USE DATABASE
FLD       NAME       TYPE     WIDTH     DEC     (Computer's Response)

001     NAME         C         020
002     ADDRESS      C         040
003     PHONE        C         008

**TOTAL**                               00069

                        Screen 1-8
```

You should notice that the computer has added .DBF to the FILENAME of the database. Note also that the "TOTAL" is one more than the visible total of number of characters used.

Database

.DBF is a 'filetype.' For other files we will encounter later, the computer will also add the filetype. The filetype 'tells' the computer how to "deal" with the file. The date of last update is the date that was 'keyed in' when we entered dBASE II. Each time the database is 'entered' a date is keyed in. If something is changed in the database the date of last update will be changed. If you enter a RETURN — the alternative to entering a date — the date of last update shows as 00/00/00. The item 'total' appearing at the bottom indicates the number of characters (plus 1) in a record. This is the record size indicator and its significance will be discussed later.

Now that we have 'used' B:FONEBOOK to view the structure we made, let's move on to the major 'use' for databases: the storage and retrieval of information. Say we want to retrieve some of the information we have stored so we can look at it. One way to look at the information is to type DISPLAY ALL after a DOT PROMPT. DISPLAY ALL is the dBASE II command that displays the contents of the database. The result of this command is shown in Screen 1-9.

```
. USE B:FONEBOOK
. DISPLAY ALL

00001      Byers, Robert A Sr     9999 Glencrest, Standale       555-9242
00002      Byers, Robert A Jr     48 N. Catalina, Pasadena       555-9540
00003      Cassidy, Butch         4800 Rimrock Ct, Sunland       878-1121
00004      Evans, Sydney H.       398 S. Calif. Blvd. Encino     998-1234
00005      Goose, Sil E.          21809 Cottage Ln, Montecito    675-1212
00006      Hedman, Gene           139 Luxury Dr. Bev. Hills      987-6543
00007      Maori, Stanislas       2800 Oak St. #344 Red. Bch.    324-8529
00008      Robertson, James       5892 Glencrest, Standale       997-2741
```

Screen 1-9

The left hand column displays the automatically assigned RECORD NUMBER we discussed previously. If you do not want the record number displayed, type DISPLAY ALL OFF instead of DISPLAY ALL. The computer will generate the same display except the record numbers will not be shown.

Earlier in this chapter, we gave some examples of the kinds of things the computer can easily do. One of these examples had to do with a phone number on a scrap of paper. The dBASE II command DISPLAY will give us the owner of that phone number (if it is in the database). To accomplish this, we must tell the computer what we want it to do in a way that it will understand. The computer may be fast, but it's not particularly bright.

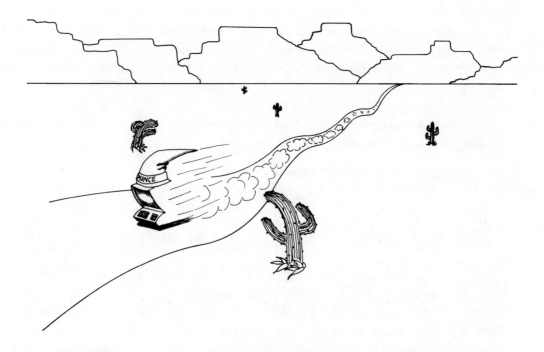

So, we use the dBASE II DISPLAY command to give us the 'owner' of the telephone number on the scrap of paper we found. The transaction looks like this:

.DISPLAY FOR PHONE='998-1234'

00004   Evans, Sydney H.   398 S. Calif. Blvd. Encino   998-1234

Database

This looks very straightforward and it is. The word PHONE is the FIELDNAME of the FIELD (column) containing the phone numbers. What you are really telling the computer with the short instruction above is: look through the entire database and display each record containing the characters '998-1234' in the phone column.

The apostrophes at each end of the phone number are important. If they were not there the computer wouldn't know what to do except to tell you that you made an error.

These apostrophes are called DELIMITERS. They are there to identify to the computer the beginning and the end of what is called a 'CHARACTER STRING'. What is contained between the apostrophes is specifically, to the letter and the space, what you are looking for.

Phone numbers are character strings because we identified the phone number field (PHONE) as a character field when we created the database. Numbers can be either numbers or characters. You must tell the computer which they are by using the delimiters. As an example, 555 is a number to the computer, while '555' is a character string. Numbers should normally be entered as characters unless they are to be used in arithmetic.

As another example, let's find everyone who lives in Standale. This transaction is as follows:

.DISPLAY FOR 'Standale'$ADDRESS

| 00001 | Byers, Robert A Sr | 9999 Glencrest, Standale | 555-9242 |
| 00008 | Robertson, James | 5892 Glencrest, Standale | 997-2741 |

Just as before, the character string is enclosed in apostrophes. This example, however, looks a little more exotic. The dollar sign is a sort of shorthand for 'contained in'. What we tell the machine to do is: look through the entire database and display each record that contains the characters 'Standale' in the address column. If there is a Standale Avenue somewhere in that field of the database, that record is reported along with the two Standale 'town' addresses reported. Again, what it's looking for is a *sequence of characters*. To further illustrate the character sequence concept we tell the computer to:

.DISPLAY FOR 'STANDALE'$ADDRESS
♦
.

The computer responds with a DOT PROMPT. This means there are no records with the character string STANDALE in the address field. The two character strings Standale and STANDALE are different. The first uses lower case while the latter uses all upper case. In this example you and I would know they mean the same thing, but the computer doesn't. The computer's interpretation is very literal.

As another example of the computer's literal interpretation, let's tell the computer to display all the records containing the CHARACTER STRING 'Robert'. The computer's response is shown in Screen 1-10.

```
. DISPLAY FOR 'Robert'$NAME

00001      Byers, Robert A Sr      9999 Glencrest, Standale      555-9242
00002      Byers, Robert A Jr      48 N. Catalina, Pasadena      555-9540
00008      Robertson, James        5892 Glencrest, Standale      997-2741


                           Screen 1-10
```

This is a graphic example of a character string search where the computer gave more information than we thought we asked it for. The point here: *it did exactly what it was told.* In this case, we wanted a display of everyone whose first name was Robert. This would have been obtained by using ', Robert' instead of 'Robert' in the instruction. This is because 'Robert' as a first name always follows a comma.

To remove a little more of the mystique (if it even had any) from computer database operations, let's take a look at what process happens when we say DISPLAY FOR 'Standale'$ADDRESS.

● The computer 'goes' to the beginning of the database (Record 1) and looks through the ADDRESS field of Record 1 to see if the CHARACTER STRING 'Standale' is there.

- If it is there, the computer will display all of Record 1 on the video terminal.

- If it is not there, the computer will not display any part of Record 1.

- When Record 1 has been examined and either displayed on the terminal or not, the computer will proceed to examine Record 2 in exactly the same manner.

- This Record by Record examination of the ADDRESS FIELD continues until every record has been examined.

Let's recap what we've done so far. We've learned a little of the terminology, that databases can be likened to things we use everyday, and that databases and computers can't do anything you can't do without them — if you have lots and lots and lots of time.

Up to this point, a paper and pencil would have been much faster, cheaper and you wouldn't have needed to learn any computer terminology. Bear in mind, however, that this list would easily be 80, 800, or 8,000 names long. Examples in this book never have more than 15 records (in the interest of conserving paper and your interest). In order to appreciate what this particular computer technology can do for you, you should think of these examples as small sections of databases containing hundreds or thousands of records.

This entire process is very much like making a table with paper and pencil.

- You must plan your layout, decide what information is to go in which columns, and determine the physical size of each column.

- Then you enter all of the information.

- It is only after this is all accomplished that you can actually use the table for its intended purpose. In this chapter we only 'used' the database one way — we looked at it, i.e., DISPLAYed it.

The process of making a table on paper is directly analagous to the computer database process. The database must be planned. Data must be entered. Then, and only then, can you use it to do something.

The nice part about all this is that you can accomplish this knowing nothing about the internal working of the computer. All you have to do is to follow the rules. It's a little like learning to drive an automobile with an automatic as opposed to a manual transmission.

The language you use to 'talk' to the computer is a VERY limited English. Nearly all commercially available databases have 'English' vocabularies of less than a hundred words. Furthermore, unlike non-computer English, there are no 'special' cases. Each English word means what it meant the last time it was used. Each English word in the computer's vocabulary has a very narrow meaning with no room for interpretation. The meaning will be ONE of the common English meanings for the word.

Finally, you have nothing to worry about. While you are learning, you can't break the computer and if you aren't quite sure about something — just try a few things and see if they work. Probably the hardest thing to learn is that there is really nothing difficult about working with the computer. It should be an easy thing to master. You will use only a limited vocabulary and no difficult physical coordination (such as using an automobile clutch) is required.

Database

CHAPTER II

SIMPLE DATABASE USES:
HOW THEY WORK

Now that you're familiar with what a database is, we are ready to discuss some simple database uses and how they work. We have already discussed one simple use: DISPLAY. With it, we looked at the structure and contents of a very simple database.

In this chapter, we will learn to change the database — by both adding and deleting information, to produce standard reports and to index and sort database contents. We will also CREATE a slightly more complex database than B:FONEBOOK of Chapter 1.

So, we have discussed two simple ways to USE the database:

● a way to look at its structure, and
● ways to view all or selective parts of the database contents.

The next significant database use process that will concern us is change. It is very important to know we can easily accommodate necessary changes.

Continuing with the personal telephone directory example, we would expect that we could easily 'erase' names, addresses and phone numbers and enter new ones in their places.

This is exactly the case. This capability is necessary for several reasons. Mistakes are made while entering data — the wrong address and phone number are entered for a name, words are misspelled, numbers are left out, etc. People move and telephone numbers and addresses change. Others get married and their names change. Some people disappear from our lives — others enter. If the world were truly static and nothing changed, the value of databases would be significantly lower. The world, however, is doing everything but standing still. It is changing at an ever faster pace and this makes the value of databases considerable.

CHANGE

There are generally three kinds of change the computer can accommodate:

- One is to add or delete entire records

- Another is to change the contents of a record

- The last is to change the structure of the database by adding or erasing entire fields (columns).

DELETE RECORDS

Deleting a record is a two step process. This provides a safeguard against accidental erasure. In dBASE II, two separate commands are used: DELETE and PACK. To illustrate the procedure we will erase the record for Sydney Evans (RECORD 4). The transaction with the computer is illustrated by Screen 2-1.

```
.DELETE FOR NAME='Evans, Sydney H'
00001 DELETION(S)
.DISPLAY FOR *
00004     *Evans, Sydney H.      398 S. Calif. Blvd., Encino        998-1234
.PACK
PACK COMPLETE 00007 RECORDS COPIED


                            Screen 2-1
```

We tell the computer 'delete the record that contains Sydney Evans.' The DELETE command places a mark (*) in front of the record we want to remove. The computer tells us [with (*)] that it has marked one record for deletion. At this point, the record is still in the database. If it had found another Sydney Evans, the response would have been '00002 DELETIONS', a clue to us that something unexpected had occured.

The DISPLAY FOR command tells the computer to display the records marked for removal. The computer displays a single record, the one marked for elimination. Notice that the * symbol appears between the RECORD NUMBER and the RECORD.

The command PACK actually removes the record. This eliminates all the records marked by the DELETE command and renumbers all remaining record numbers.

If we now display the entire database, we see that the record for Sydney Evans is now gone. There are now only 7 records, and the record that was formerly number 5 is now number 4 and so forth. The revised database is shown in Screen 2-2.

00001	Byers, Robert A Sr	9999 Glencrest, Standale	555-9242
00002	Byers, Robert A Jr	48 N. Catalina, Pasadena	555-9540
00003	Cassidy, Butch	4800 Rimrock Ct., Sunland	878-1121
00004	Goose, Sil E.	21809 Cottage Ln., Montecito	675-1212
00005	Hedman, Gene	139 Luxury Dr., Bev. Hills	987-6543
00006	Maori, Stanislas	2800 Oak St. #344, Red. Bch.	324-8529
00007	Robertson, James	5892 Glencrest, Standale	997-2741

Screen 2-2

ADDING RECORDS (APPEND)

Adding a record to the database is a simple one step process. In dBASE II, the command to add a record is APPEND. Entering data for APPEND is exactly the same as entering data for CREATE. When the computer is told to APPEND, the computer will clear the screen and generate the display shown in Screen 2-3.

```
RECORD #00008

NAME          : ◆                            :
ADDRESS       :                                        :
PHONE         :        :


              Screen 2-3
```

To actually add the record, fill in the blanks as in the CREATE process. IT'S JUST LIKE FILLING IN A FORM WITH A TYPEWRITER. You may add as many records as you desire. To exit from APPEND press the RETURN key when the cursor is in the first position of the first field of the new record — exactly as in CREATE.

The new entry is shown in Screen 2-4. In this example we did not know the address for T. E. Deum so a RETURN was entered to advance the cursor to the PHONE field.

```
RECORD 00008

NAME          :Deum, T. E.                   :
ADDRESS       :                                        :
PHONE         :333-9194:


              Screen 2-4
```

As in the CREATE example, the computer automatically advances to the next record (Record 9) and prompts you to enter the data. Pressing the RETURN key will stop the APPEND process and have the computer respond with a dot prompt.

EDIT & REPLACE

Now, suppose we acquire an address for T. E. Deum and his phone number changes. There are two principal commands used to edit (change) the fields within a record. These are EDIT and REPLACE.

The EDIT command is similar to the APPEND command except that it does not add a record. Unlike the APPEND command, however, it requires a knowledge of the RECORD number. It is one of the few dBASE II commands requiring a knowledge of record numbers. A record may be EDITed without that knowledge but a two step process is required. Use of the EDIT command is described below. To invoke the EDIT function, type EDIT followed by the desired record number after a DOT PROMPT.

.EDIT 8

EDIT is similar to APPEND, except that instead of displaying empty FIELDS as in APPEND, the contents of the desired record are displayed. The cursor will appear, as in APPEND, in the first position of the first field. In this example, we will add the address and change the phone number.

To change the address, we must move the cursor to the ADDRESS field. This requires knowledge of something we haven't done before. Cursor movement like this requires use of the CONTROL or CTRL key.

THE CONTROL KEY

The CONTROL key is not found on the ordinary typewriter. It is used in a similar manner to the SHIFT key on the typewriter. The SHIFT key gives a 'second meaning' to each typewriter key. Holding the shift key while pressing the 'h' key produces a capital 'H' on the typewriter. The CONTROL (or CTRL) key provides a 'third meaning' to some of the keys. For example, while the control key is depressed, the 'X' key will advance the cursor one field each time the 'X' is pressed. This is spoken as CONTROL X. It is often written as ^X (or CTRL X or CODE X). The effect of some of the CONTROL keys is summarized in Table 2-1.

CONTROL KEY	EFFECT
X	Moves cursor 1 field ahead
E	Moves cursor 1 field back
D	Moves cursor 1 space ahead
S	Moves cursor 1 space back
Y	Erases field contents
V	Inserts characters at cursor location
G	Erases character at cursor location
W	Exit from EDIT

Table 2-1. Some Control Key Characteristics

Now that we understand some CONTROL key functions, we can proceed with editing RECORD 8. Since before our discussion of CONTROL keys we had typed EDIT 8 in response to the DOT PROMPT, Record 8 is now displayed on our screen, with the cursor positioned in the NAME field.

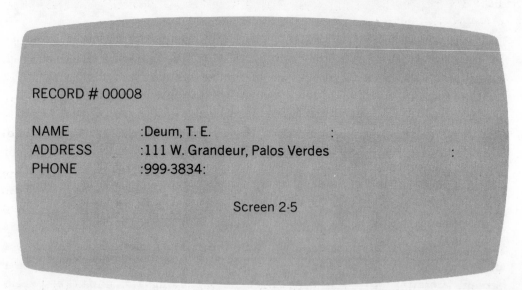

```
RECORD # 00008

NAME          :Deum, T. E.                        :
ADDRESS       :111 W. Grandeur, Palos Verdes              :
PHONE         :999-3834:


                    Screen 2-5
```

To move the cursor to the ADDRESS field, press CTRL X (^). This moves the cursor to the first character position of the ADDRESS field. Enter the address as shown in Screen 2-5. Entering a return will position the cursor to the beginning of the PHONE field. To change the phone number just type the new number directly over the old one.

When the '4' was entered in the phone number above, the computer automatically exited from the EDIT command. It did this because we had entered the last character in the last field of the last record of the database. If this had not been the last field of the last record, we would have had to purposefully exit from edit. This is done with CONTROL 'W'. In this case, 'W' is for 'write'. ^W asks the computer to 'write' the new information or structure onto the disk. The act of 'exiting' says you are finished with your changes and what is done should be 'written' to the disk for permanent storage.

The other change command, REPLACE, allows selective change of one or more records based on some criteria. With REPLACE, you change the content of one or more fields by 'telling' the computer the fieldnames, the new contents, and the criteria for making a change.

As an example, suppose the last entry, T. E. Deum, has moved. He has a new address and a new telephone number. To change the telephone number and address with the REPLACE command, the transaction looks like this:

```
.REPLACE PHONE WITH '222-6661',ADDRESS WITH '200 Splendid Ave, Escondido'
FOR NAME='Deum, T. E.'
00001 REPLACEMENT(S)
```

The computer's response of '00001 REPLACEMENT(S)' even though two fields were changed (replaced) refers to the number of records changed by the command. The command changed both the telephone number and the address to the new information.

Both EDIT and REPLACE have extensive uses for modifying the contents of the database. EDIT is what is called a fullscreen operation. The database record, in a sense, IS ON THE SCREEN and can be changed by typing new information right over the old. REPLACE may be used to automatically replace certain data with new data according to criteria established by the user. The change is made in the computer but is not actually seen on the screen. If visual confirmation is desired, a separate display command must be used.

The personal telephone book exercise covers familiar territory we can all relate to. It is, however, very limited. It does not begin to be enough material to demonstrate the full range of computer database capabilities.

37

Simple Database Uses:
How They Work

So, it is time to begin our second database project. Our new database will be capable of demonstrating more facets of computer database capability. The concept, if not the actuality, behind this database is familiar to us all. It is based on the needs of a retail store inventory. In this case, we will conduct an annual inventory similar to what might be undertaken by the proprietor of a very small liquor store.

What items might be of interest to the liquor store owner? Likely items include:

> Type of Liquor
> Brand Name
> Size
> Amount of Stock on Hand
> Wholesale Cost
> Retail Price

These items then become the columns (fields) needed in our new database. Our next 3 steps are all part of one process which defines the database form and arrangement.

1. We assign FIELDNAMES
2. Assign category to each field (character, numeric, logical)
3. Decide the size (width) of each field

- In this example, the fieldname for the column containing the type of liquor is LIQUOR. It is a character field that is 10 spaces wide.

- The column for the brandnames has the fieldname BRAND, is a character field, and is 20 spaces wide.

- That for container size is SIZE, is a character field, and is 7 spaces wide.

- The amount of stock is QUANTITY, a number field, and is 3 digits wide. This allows up to 999 containers of each size of each brand in the inventory of this small store.

- The last two fields, called COST and PRICE, are also number fields. These two fields will contain decimal values, however, and are entered in a slightly different manner. For both, we will allow 3 digits to the left of the decimal place, and 2 digits to the right. This will allow a maximum of 999.99. The field width for each of these two fields is SIX (5 digits plus the decimal point).

We have exactly the same problem in choosing a FILENAME (title) for this database as we did in the example of the personal telephone directory. Liquor Store Inventory is too large and contains blank spaces. We will choose to use INVENTRY as the filename. It is descriptive, and has eight letters.

CREATE A DATABASE

The process we have just been through is shown in Screen 2-6. The database (file) INVENTRY will be placed on the B disk drive.

```
. CREATE
ENTER FILENAME:  B:INVENTRY
ENTER RECORD STRUCTURE AS FOLLOWS:
FIELD              NAME,TYPE,WIDTH,DECIMAL PLACES
001                LIQUOR,C,10
002                BRAND,C,20
003                SIZE,C,7
004                QUANTITY,N,3
005                COST,N,6,2
006                PRICE,N,6,2
007

INPUT DATA NOW? Y


                        Screen 2-6
```

With your Y (yes) response, the computer begins prompting you to enter the data for the first record. The video display is shown in Screen 2-7.

```
RECORD # 00001


LIQUOR                    :
BRAND          :                    :
SIZE           :          :
QUANTITY       :          :
COST           :          :
PRICE          :          :



                    Screen 2-7
```

We will now enter the data into the database INVENTRY. A representative record is depicted by Screen 2-8.

```
RECORD # 00001

LIQUOR          :SCOTCH:
BRAND           :AULD COUNTRY:
SIZE            :QUART:
QUANTITY        : 23:
COST            : 5.59:
PRICE           : 9.31:


                   Screen 2-8
```

This process will continue, filling in record by record, until all of the data for the fifteen records has been entered. A RETURN at the beginning of Record 16 gets us out of the data entry mode.

NOTES ON ENTERING DATA

Data entry begins at the left hand colon for each field. If the field is a character field, the data will remain at the left hand colon, just as it would if you were typing it on a piece of paper. This is called *left justification*.

For number fields, the data is entered beginning at the left hand colon just as for character fields. However, when you press the return key (telling the computer that you have finished entering the field), the computer will move the number over against the right hand colon, just as you would if typing the numbers into a column. This is called *right justification*. The computer will right justify number fields.

If you attempt to enter a letter into a numeric field, dBASE II will not allow it. The letter will not be accepted and the terminal will sound an audible alarm.

The data entry process can go on until the inventory is completed (or there is enough data for our example). Our sample database B:INVENTRY has 6 FIELDS and 15 RECORDS.

In order to do something with the database we must first tell the computer to use the database. In this case we use it by requesting that it LIST B:INVENTRY. The complete contents of our sample database B:INVENTRY are shown in Screen 2-9.

```
. USE B:INVENTRY
. LIST

00001   SCOTCH    AULD COUNTRY              QUART     23   5.59    9.31
00002   SCOTCH    AULD COUNTRY              2 LITER    7   9.78   16.30
00003   SCOTCH    AULD COUNTRY              PINT      88   2.74    4.56
00004   VODKA     REAL RUSSIAN              QUART     35   3.78    6.30
00005   VODKA     REAL RUSSIAN              2 LITER    9   7.95   13.25
00006   VODKA     REAL RUSSIAN              PINT      75   1.49    2.48
00007   WHISKEY   SOUTHERN RYE              QUART     32   5.11    8.51
00008   WHISKEY   OLD WYOMING               PINT      44   1.98    3.30
00009   WHISKEY   OLD WYOMING               QUART     19   5.29    8.81
00010   WHISKEY   THE NEW SOUTH             QUART      4   7.49   12.48
00011   BOURBON   SOUTHERN ARISTOCRACY      PINT       5   0.99    1.65
00012   BOURBON   SOUTHERN ARISTOCRACY      FIFTH     22   1.78    2.96
00013   BOURBON   SOUTHERN ARISTOCRACY      QUART     21   3.50    5.83
00014   BOURBON   SOUTHERN ARISTOCRACY      1/2 GAL    3   6.89   11.48
00015   BOURBON   SOUTHERN ARISTOCRACY      2 LITER    5   6.47   10.78
```

Screen 2-9

Simple Database Uses:
How They Work

One of the objectives of an inventory is to determine the amount of capital tied up in inventory. When we finish an inventory in the conventional way, with pencil and paper, we can compute the value of the inventory by multiplying each quantity by the corresponding cost and adding the results. If the inventory is done with a microcomputer and a database management system, such as dBASE II, we can get the same result almost immediately. The system can do this for us. From this example we can begin to see the power of the database.

The dBASE II command requesting the value of the inventory looks like this:

.SUM COST*QUANTITY
1305.49

We have asked for the sum (total) of cost times quantity. The asterisk '*' symbol requests multiplication of the computer. The result of this operation (1305.49) is shown just below the command. The computer applies the above command to the entire database.

Suppose you only wanted to know how much capital is invested in scotch. The transaction is shown below.

.SUM COST*QUANTITY FOR LIQUOR='SCOTCH'
438.15

Now suppose you want to know the investment in quarts of scotch. The command (and the result) is shown below. In this example, we see another peculiarity of the computer. AND must be preceeded and followed by a period so it looks like '.AND.'

.SUM COST*QUANTITY FOR LIQUOR='SCOTCH'.AND.SIZE='QUART'
128.57

Simple computations such as these are only the beginning of information readily available via simple database transactions. You can actually get whole reports, organized to use and display your information according to your specific needs, with just two commands.

STANDARD REPORTS

dBASE II has a built-in 'report generation' feature called REPORT. Many reports can be prepared on the basis of this feature alone. REPORT can be prepared directly from the computer keyboard and the report 'form' can be saved for future use.

After a DOT PROMPT, type REPORT. The computer will ask you a series of questions called PROMPTS. This is just like filling in a form. The answers are used by the computer to prepare the report.

- The first prompt is a request for a REPORT FORM NAME. This is another kind of FILENAME, similar to the FILENAME for the database. Filenames for report forms follow the same rules as filenames for databases. They must begin with the disk drive identifier, followed by a colon, followed by eight or fewer letters and numbers. Since we are using the database B:INVENTRY, we elect to call the report form B:INVENTRY also.

You may wonder how the computer can tell the difference between B:INVENTRY (the database) and B:INVENTRY (the report form). In a database management system, there are different 'types' of files and the computer has its own labeling system to keep them separately identified. The system adds .DBF (database file) to the names of files such as B:FONEBOOK and B:INVENTRY. In this case, because of the process we are going through, the system knows to identify this file as a form file, adding .FRM to our filename. We can still call it B:INVENTRY because the computer does its own distinguishing between B:INVENTRY.DBF and B:INVENTRY.FRM.

After you enter the FILENAME for the report, the computer begins prompting you to supply the information it needs to prepare the report. A report of this type is essentially a form where the computer fills in the blanks.

If a report with this filename had previously been generated, when we typed REPORT and then FILENAME, the computer would simply generate the report. We are, however, asking it to report for the first time, so first we have to answer its PROMPTS to generate a proper form.

- The second prompt selects from a menu of standard options including left margin choice, number of lines per page and page width. Pressing the return key indicates you're not interested in changing any options, content instead with the 'standard' format.

- The 'PAGE HEADING?' prompt asks if you want to have a heading (title) printed on each page of the report.

- A yes will cause 'ENTER PAGE HEADING' to appear. You might type LIQUOR STORE INVENTORY.

- The next prompt allows a choice of single (N) or double (Y) spacing.

- The next prompt asks if totals are required.

  - If they are, next prompt is — ARE SUBTOTALS REQUIRED?

  - If Yes, next prompt is — ENTER SUBTOTALS FIELD, i.e., which field do you wish to subtotal on? In this case, we want subtotals for each kind of LIQUOR.

- The next prompt is a choice: SUMMARY REPORT ONLY? If N, you want a FULL REPORT. The example below is a FULL REPORT. A "SUMMARY" would show only the kind of liquor and the subtotals.

- Since the report can be printed as well as displayed on the terminal, you are asked if the page should be ejected after each subtotal. The computer is really asking you if you want each subtotaled category printed on a separate page (or group of pages). In our example, a yes would cause the report to be printed on four separate pages.

- The next prompt asks for a SUBTOTAL HEADING. This is only applicable if a heading is necessary in addition to the contents of the subtotal field. In this example, additional text is not needed so the RETURN KEY is pressed.

- Next, the computer needs to be told how many columns there are in the report and what is to be in each column. To acquire the information it needs, it will prompt you for the size and content of each column. Columns are defined one at a time and left to right.

The content of a column may be either a FIELDNAME or an expression such as COST*QUANTITY. The report will contain the contents of that field or the result of the expression.

When you have finished defining all the columns that you want, press the RETURN KEY when prompted to enter the column width. This ends the form generation task and saves the report for future use.

The transaction we have just been through is shown on Screen 2-10 below:

```
. REPORT
ENTER REPORT FORM NAME:  B:INVENTRY
ENTER OPTIONS, M=LEFT MARGIN, L=LINE/PAGE, W=PAGE WIDTH
PAGE HEADING? (Y/N) Y
ENTER PAGE HEADING:  LIQUOR STORE INVENTORY
DOUBLE SPACE REPORT? (Y/N) N
TOTALS REQUIRED IN REPORT? Y
SUBTOTALS IN REPORT? (Y/N) Y
ENTER SUBTOTALS FIELD:  LIQUOR
SUMMARY REPORT ONLY? (Y/N) N
EJECT PAGE AFTER SUBTOTALS? (Y/N) N
ENTER SUBTOTAL HEADING:
COL        WIDTH,CONTENTS
001      20,BRAND
ENTER HEADNG:  BRAND
002      7,SIZE
ENTER HEADNG:  SIZE
003      3,QUANTITY
ENTER HEADING:  QTY
ARE SUBTOTALS REQUIRED? (Y/N) Y
004      6,COST
ENTER HEADING:  COST
ARE TOTALS REQUIRED? (Y/N) N
005      7,COST*QUANTITY
ENTER HEADING:  INVEST
ARE TOTALS REQUIRED? (Y/N) Y
006
                     Screen 2-10
```

Completion of this initial work means that any time you ask the computer to .REPORT and enter the filename B:INVENTRY, the computer will produce the report shown in Figure 2-1. If you ask it .REPORT TO PRINT instead of just .REPORT, a printed copy will be produced.

PAGE NO. 00001
09/15/81

LIQUOR STORE INVENTORY

BRAND		QTY	COST	INVEST
* SCOTCH				
AULD COUNTRY	QUART	23	5.59	128.57
AULD COUNTRY	1/2 LIT	7	9.78	68.46
AULD COUNTRY	PINT	88	2.74	241.12
** SUBTOTAL **		118		438.15
* VODKA				
REAL RUSSIAN	QUART	35	3.78	132.30
REAL RUSSIAN	1/2 LIT	9	7.95	71.55
REAL RUSSIAN	PINT	75	1.49	111.75
** SUBTOTAL **		119		315.60
* WHISKEY				
SOUTHERN RYE	QUART	32	5.11	163.52
OLD WYOMING	PINT	44	1.98	87.12
OLD WYOMING	QUART	19	5.29	100.51
THE NEW SOUTH	QUART	4	7.49	29.96
** SUBTOTAL **		99		381.11
* BOURBON				
SOUTHERN ARISTOCRACY	PINT	5	0.99	4.95
SOUTHERN ARISTOCRACY	FIFTH	22	1.78	39.16
SOUTHERN ARISTOCRACY	QUART	21	3.50	73.50
SOUTHERN ARISTOCRACY	1/2 GAL	3	6.89	20.67
SOUTHERN ARISTOCRACY	1/2 LIT	5	6.47	32.35
** SUBTOTAL **		56		170.63
** TOTAL **		392		1305.49

Figure 2-1. Computer Report On Liquor Store Inventory

So what have we done? What might we have done? If we had actually conducted an inventory of a small liquor store, most likely we would have used pencil, paper and adding machine. Now we can do it with a computer database management system. The results will be available within minutes of inventory completion. We significantly reduce the opportunity for error by eliminating the adding machine. And, all of this is possible without knowing anything about a computer, computer programming, or database management systems. All we have to do is follow the same steps we have been through in the last few pages. If you think about it, this example is pretty remarkable: All of this for two commands — CREATE and REPORT.

Maybe then, to give us a different feel for what is in our inventory, we might want to reorganize our listing of inventory items. It is very possible that our stocking scheme keys on the sizes of different kinds and brands of liquor. Within the database, we have the ability to index or sort. INDEXING and SORTING are similar in concept but entirely different in application.

INDEXING OR SORTING

If we SORT a database, we actually 'physically' rearrange the database.

Simple Database Uses:
How They Work

A non-computer example of this is to sort a deck of cards. We can arrange the cards in many different ways, but only in one way at a time. Suppose we arrange the cards in suits, and then in value within the suits. If this is the case, and we want the Jack of Diamonds, we know where to look. If we take the cards and rearrange them (SORT) by value, we have an entirely different sequence of cards, but we will still know where to find the Jack of Diamonds.

A very clever way to accomplish the same result is to INDEX the cards. This leaves the physical arrangement of the database in its original order. INDEX creates a separate list that describes the location of the item we want. To illustrate this, we will again consider the deck of cards. On a sheet of paper, make a list of each card in the order shown in Figure 2-2.

SUIT	CARD	POSITION
Spades	Ace	
	King	
	Queen	
	.	
	Two	
Hearts	Ace	
	.	
	Two	
Diamonds	.	
Clubs	.	

Figure 2-2

You now have an ordered list of the 52 cards in the deck. Now, take the cards and shuffle them well.

Take the first card from the top of the deck. Locate the card in the list and write the number '1' under 'POSITION' across from the card description (Spades......Ace........1). Place the card on the table and repeat this operation until you have entered all of the cards in the deck.

48

The list is now an INDEX. Any card can be located by finding it in the list and counting card by card from the bottom of the deck. For example, if the Jack of Diamonds has the number 10 written after it on the list, it is the 10th card from the bottom of the deck. The card location numbers on the list are called POINTERS.

We can also make a list that describes another possible card arrangement: the cards arranged by face value and suit within value. Such an arrangement is shown in Figure 2-3.

CARD	SUIT	POSITION
Ace	Spades	
	Hearts	
	Clubs	
	Diamonds	
King	Spades	
	Hearts	
	.	
	.	
	.	
	Etc.	
Etc.		

Figure 2-3. Another Card List

If we go through our deck again and list card positions, we will end up with two lists which describe the same physical arrangement of the card deck. As long as we do not change the order of the cards, we can find cards quickly using either INDEX.

Another common example of INDEXES and POINTERS is found in the Library. If you go to the library knowing you want a particular book, you can find it in one of two ways: either wander around starting with the first shelf, and continuing a shelf at a time until you find the book, or use the card catalog which tells you which shelf the book is on. The card catalog is a multiple index. There are INDEX cards to locate books based on title, author, and subject. Each card contains POINTERS, based on what you already know, to tell you where to find the book.

Depending on the type of database you have, you can maintain one or more indexes on the records. With the kind of database we are using, we can use the database B:INVENTRY and make an index on the size of the liquor bottle. When we do this we must have an INDEX FILE where the desired order of the records is stored. In this example, we call the index file B:SIZINDEX. We first use our inventory file B:INVENTRY and then we can index on the size. Size, of course, doesn't really mean anything to the computer. The index groups the records by an 'alphabetical' ordering of the contents of the size field. This groups all like sizes together because they start with the same letter and are spelled the same.

This operation and the result is shown as Screen 2-11.

```
.USE B:INVENTRY
.INDEX ON SIZE TO B:SIZINDEX
00015 RECORDS INDEXED
.DISPLAY ALL

00014   BOURBON   SOUTHERN ARISTOCRACY   1/2 GAL    3   6.89   11.48
00002   SCOTCH    AULD COUNTRY           1/2 LIT    7   9.78   16.30
00005   VODKA     REAL RUSSIAN           1/2 LIT    9   7.95   13.25
00015   BOURBON   SOUTHERN ARISTOCRACY   1/2 LIT    5   6.47   10.78
00012   BOURBON   SOUTHERN ARISTOCRACY   FIFTH     22   1.78    2.96
00003   SCOTCH    AULD COUNTRY           PINT      88   2.74    4.56
00006   VODKA     REAL RUSSIAN           PINT      75   1.49    2.48
00008   WHISKEY   OLD WYOMING            PINT      44   1.98    3.30
00011   BOURBON   SOUTHERN ARISTOCRACY   PINT       5   0.99    1.65
00001   SCOTCH    AULD COUNTRY           QUART     23   5.59    9.31
00004   VODKA     REAL RUSSIAN           QUART     35   3.78    6.30
00007   WHISKEY   SOUTHERN RYE           QUART     32   5.11    8.51
00009   WHISKEY   OLD WYOMING            QUART     19   5.29    8.81
00010   WHISKEY   THE NEW SOUTH          QUART      4   7.49   12.48
00013   BOURBON   SOUTHERN ARISTOCRACY   QUART     21   3.50    5.83
```

Screen 2-11

By making use of INDEX and an INDEX FILE, we leave the physical database in the order of its original data entry. You can tell by looking at the record number column which reflects where each entry is in the database.

What has happened here is very similar to the example of the card deck and the lists. The display is controlled by the INDEX file B:SIZINDEX instead of the order in which the data was entered. One of the really nice features of INDEX is that you don't have to be concerned about the order in which records are entered. The computer can quickly arrange them into nearly any sequence or grouping you might desire.

In these first two chapters, we have discussed some basic concepts and workings of microcomputer database management systems. This basic orientation and beginning 'hands-on' experience is the foundation for bigger and better things.

These systems use the speed of the computer to perform tasks that, in the past, we performed manually with the aid of 'paper databases'. We used the analogy of the paper database to illustrate how a database management system works and to introduce the terminology.

- The database management system provides a mechanism for storing data in the computer, for retrieving, manipulating, and changing that data, and for preparing reports based upon that data.

- The modern microcomputer database systems do not require that the user either have or acquire a technical background.

- For the most part, they have been successful in adapting the computer to the needs of the user rather than forcing the user to adapt to the computer. These systems will eventually become the basis for 'everyday' use of the computer.

Simple Database Uses:
How They Work

CHAPTER III

WHAT ABOUT HARDWARE SYSTEMS?

In the first two chapters, we did what is usually referred to as a 'survey of the field.' We learned that a microcomputer and a database management system (DBMS) are easy to use and to understand. Our brief sample of how database management systems work and what they can do for us will be expanded in the following chapters. In the chapters to come we will go over this same material in much more detail. And, of course, we will also introduce new material.

In this chapter we will provide an introduction to microcomputer hardware systems. In order to use a database system you must have a computer. (Although — as we said earlier — you will be able to understand and follow the material without having a computer). In case you are unfamiliar with computers, this brief discussion will include the basic elements of computer systems and then indicate what you will need to be able to use a database system. As you will see in this chapter, as well as later chapters, your database needs have a significant effect on the computer hardware that you need.

A typical microcomputer system is diagrammed in Figure 3-1.

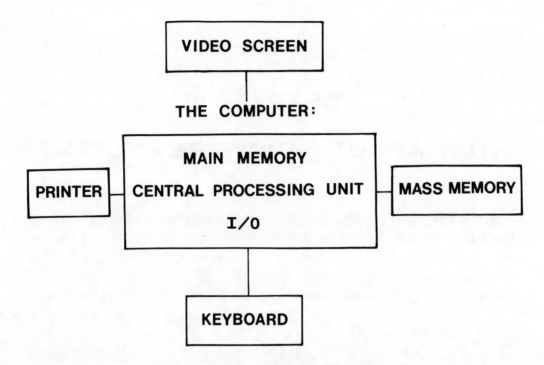

Figure 3-1. A Typical Microcomputer

The diagram above describes any computer system: it could be a microcomputer or a very large computer. The computer itself consists of what is inside the box labeled computer — the central processing unit, the main memory and the I/O (input/output). The other four boxes — video screen, mass memory, printer, and keyboard are called peripherals.

THE 'COMPUTER' (Consisting of — Central Processing Unit
Main Memory
Input/Output)

The central processing unit is usually referred to as the CPU. It is the device that actually does the 'computing'. For it to function, however, it must have MAIN MEMORY. Main memory is used directly by the CPU.

Advertisements for microcomputers usually say something like

"BUY A 24K Cucumber IV"

The 24K refers to the amount of main memory in something called BYTES.
A BYTE is the amount of memory needed to store a typewriter character
such as 'm' or '$'. 24K usually means 24,000. In a computer memory it
actually means 24,576. A 24K computer system has 24,576 BYTES of main
memory.

Main memory is relatively expensive when compared to mass memory.
When you purchase a computer, you will want to select the amount of main
memory with some care. The database system you select will require a
minimum amount of main memory. *You will need to acquire at least that
amount of main memory for your computer system.*

I/O stands for input/output. It is the means which connects the computer
to the outside world. In this case the outside world consists of the
peripherals. You might reasonably assume that I/O is a standard feature
like tires on a car. This is not always true — computer I/O often costs extra.

For microcomputers however, cost is a relative consideration. None of the components of a microcomputer system are very expensive.

THE PERIPHERALS

Computers do not always require peripheral devices. For most database uses, however, all but one of the peripherals shown in Figure 1 are required. That is, mass memory, video screen, and keyboard are mandatory. For some uses, the printer is also a must. For other uses, the printer can be optional. It is always useful.

KEYBOARDS; MONITORS; TERMINALS

The keyboard device is similar to a typewriter keyboard. It is used to communicate with the computer. The computer communicates with you by means of the video screen. The keyboard and video screen may be separate devices. When they are separate, video is supplied by a television like device called a monitor. The keyboard and video screen are often incorporated into a single device. This is often referred to as a computer terminal, a video terminal, or sometimes just CRT.

Whether you have a terminal or keyboard and monitor usually depends upon the brand of microcomputer system you own. In this book we often refer to a terminal for convenience. There is no practical difference between a video terminal and a keyboard with separate monitor. Typical video screens can display 24 lines of 80 characters at a time. Some display somewhat less and others somewhat more. The keyboard and video screen are extremely important from a subjective point of view: these devices are your means of interaction with the computer. You 'talk' to the computer via keyboard; the computer 'talks' to you via the video screen.

MASS MEMORY

Mass memory is where most of your information is stored for microcomputer system use. It is the means to economically augment the computer's main memory. Mass memory is significantly less expensive than main memory. It is also significantly (more than a thousand times) slower. When power is turned off main memory is erased while mass memory is not. Mass memory must be deliberately changed.

56

Mass memory is used to store the information you want to save, much the same as an audio tape is used to save 'memories' of sounds. Mass storage systems are designed so the computer can easily find the information it wants. There are two kinds of mass storage commonly used by microcomputers: tape and disk.

Tape systems usually employ cassettes similar to those used for audio storage. These systems are slow and, except for some special applications are not suitable for use with database systems.

Disk systems, often referred to as direct access storage devices (DASD), are like a 'magnetic phonograph.' The information is magnetically stored on a rotating disk (hence the name) on tracks like a record. A device which is similar in concept to a tone arm (except that it has a magnetic head like those used on tape recorders) is used to 'read' and 'write' on the disk. The information is on magnetic 'tracks' that, unlike a phonograph record, are invisible to the eye.

A DISK DRIVE is the mechanism which turns the disk and transfers information to and from the disk. The computer 'knows' the location of each piece of information on each disk drive. It 'knows' this by reading the disk 'directory' for each disk. The disk directory is similar in concept to the label on a long playing record — it tells you which musical piece is located on each band on that record.

The disk drive must be controlled by a disk controller which connects to the I/O of the computer. As instructed by the CPU, the disk controller directs the movement of each disk drive's read/write head to the correct location on the magnetic disk. The disk controller provides a path for information flowing between the CPU and the disk. It also keeps the CPU informed about conditions on the disk.

For microcomputers there are two kinds of disk systems commonly used: 'floppy disk systems' and 'hard disk systems.'

FLOPPY DISK SYSTEMS

Floppy disks are often called 'floppies' or 'diskettes.' They were developed by IBM in about 1970 for use on the IBM 370 computer system. They are the most common mass storage medium for microcomputer systems. The cost of a floppy disk is about the same as the cost of a tape cassette. The cost of the floppy disk drive is usually much greater than the cost of a cassette recorder. The performance of a floppy disk system is usually an order of magnitude greater than a cassette. The performance of a 'hard' disk system is usually an order of magnitude greater than that of a floppy disk system. Most microcomputer systems for business or professional applications will have one or more floppy disk drives.

Microcomputer systems are normally equipped with from one to four disk drives. Those systems capable of working with database management systems will usually have at least one floppy disk drive. The floppy disk is a convenient way of introducing new software to the microcomputer and for transporting data or software to other microcomputers.

The floppy disk is an oxide coated mylar film which is cut into a disk resembling a 45 rpm phonograph record. The disk is packaged into a square plastic or paper envelope that has holes allowing the mylar disk to be mounted to the disk drive hub and the read/write head to have access to the disk. Another hole in the disk envelope is for index mark sensing. When the floppy disk is inserted into the disk drive, the envelope remains stationary while the mylar disk turns within it. Care must be taken to keep the mylar film clean. The mylar film must NOT be touched. Touching the film or exposing it to grease or dirt can cause severe damage to your data.

There are no universal standards for floppy disk systems. This can lead to some problems in exchanging floppy disks between systems. In order to exchange floppy disks between systems, the disk drives must be compatible.

And then, of course, there is the matter of size. Floppy disks come in 5 inch (called minifloppies) and 8 inch versions. Each can be single sided (data can be on only one side of the disk) or double sided. The density of stored information is either single density or double density (twice as much as single density). There are also 'quad density' systems.

The nominal amount of information that can be stored on each of these floppy disk types is shown in Table 3-1. These values provide a general guide to the storage capacity of 'generic' diskettes. Because of the importance of storage density to the manufacturers of computer systems and disk drives these values can vary considerably. In one sense this is unfortunate because this variation comes at the expense of inter-changeability.

	5 inch	8 inch
single sided, single density	70,000	240,000
single sided, double density	140,000	480,000
double sided, double density	280,000	960,000

Table 3-1. Floppy Disk Storage Capacity In Bytes

Most 8 inch single density disks are recorded in IBM 3740 format. This format is used by the disk drive to record the data. It was originally used by IBM for the '3740 Key to Disk Data Entry System.'

Each '3740' disk contains 77 tracks and is divided into 26 sectors. A sector is a pie shaped wedge as illustrated by the diagram in Figure 3-2. The outermost track is track 0 and the innermost track is track 76. The number of bytes stored within a sector on a track is usually independent of the track position. This means that if 100 bytes were stored in each sector of track 0 then 100 bytes will be stored in each sector of track 76. This particular arrangement allows the disk data transfer rate to be independent of track — the outer tracks move faster (inches per second) than the inner tracks.

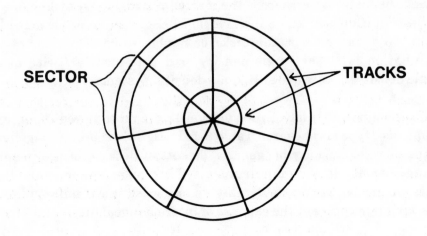

Figure 3-2. Schematic Diagram of a Disk

Unfortunately the exchangeability situation is not as good for the 5 inch mini-floppy disks. For the smaller disks, there is, as yet, no single dominant recording format. As a rule, the odds are against exchanging 5 inch disks between different microcomputer systems. It's a good idea to test compatibility between systems before making big plans to exchange information via floppy disk.

HARD DISK SYSTEMS

Even though floppy disks are used pervasively in microcomputers, 'hard' disks are certainly available and applicable. 'Hard' disk simply describes a microcomputer disk system that does not use floppies. The physical difference is that the hard disk is a rigid disk. It is made from a machined metal plate. There are hard disks that are not removable. These are called 'Winchester disks.'

The practical difference is that hard disks offer substantially higher performance than do floppy disks. They are also considerably more expensive. The storage capacity of hard disk systems starts at over a million bytes. Storage capacities of 5 to 40 million bytes and more are common.

Other performance characteristics of disk systems that you may see in advertisements are: track to track speed, average access speed, and data transfer rate. These are measures of the performance of the particular device.

Track to track means the time required by the disk drive to move the head from one track to an adjacent track. Advertised values for this capability are usually a few milliseconds. A millisecond is 1/1000 of a second.

Average access speed is the average time required to reposition the head. Specifically, it is the time required to move the head from track 1 to the last track divided by 2. It is normally several milliseconds for hard disk systems, and is almost never advertised for floppy disk drives (100 to 500 milliseconds). It is a performance specification that can be dramatically misleading and should ordinarily be ignored by you.

Data transfer rate is another specification that vendors like and that you should ignore. Data transfer rates are normally specified in hundreds of thousands to millions of bytes per second.

Double density 8 inch disks are usually recorded in IBM 34 format. Recording in a compatible format is not enough to guarantee that disks can be exchanged between microcomputers but it's a start. A good percentage of 8 inch disks can be exchanged between different microcomputer systems.

The last two specifications are carry over specifications from disk drives intended for large computers. Their application to the microcomputer is of questionable value. Of far more interest to you is whether the disk drive device is compatible with your computer—that is, what has to be done to connect the device and make it work properly with your computer. For your information, connecting the device and making it work properly is called INTEGRATION.

For the purposes of this book, mass memory is of particular importance. Microcomputer databases are normally stored on disks of one type or another. *NO* database management approach will work if you don't have adequate disk storage. Currently available microcomputers can hold only a very trivial database in main memory. Very large databases usually require a hard disk. Databases of moderate size may be contained on floppy disks of one type or another. Even large databases that are contained on hard disks may be 'backed up' on floppy disks. 'Backing up' means to make a duplicate copy of the data. This extra copy protects against disk failures and provides an economical means of transferring the database from one microcomputer to another.

THE PRINTER

A printer is always useful even if not absolutely mandatory. The particular kind of printer selected is not important to the discussion of databases.

There are two basic kinds of printers: dot matrix and daisy wheel.

- The daisy wheel printer produces a fully formed character like a typewriter does. The daisy wheel printer is usually used where letterhead quality is desired.

- The dot matrix printer uses a number of small dots to form the character.

There is a considerable variation in the print quality of dot matrix printers. Dot matrix printers are usually less expensive and of lower print quality than daisy wheel printers. They are usually significantly faster. Typical print speeds for daisy wheel printers are 40 to 50 characters a second. Print speeds for dot matrix printers are often in excess of 100 characters a second. Dot matrix print does not always reproduce on copying machines.

THE OPERATING SYSTEM

When most computers are turned on, the main memory is blank: the machine has no purpose and cannot do very much. To make the computer useful to you an OPERATING SYSTEM is needed. This system allows you and your database management system to easily use and control the computer.

Most microcomputer systems that are suitable for use with a database management system use a disk operating system (DOS). When the computer is turned on, the operating system is loaded into main memory from a disk.

This may be done automatically, or you may have to press a button on the computer. Loading the operating system is called BOOTING. Don't get worried, you will not need to know much about the operating system — now or ever — to use a database system.

The discussion in this book assumes that the operating system used is CP/M®, a popular microcomputer operating system. The only effect of a different operating system on the discussion in this book is that the rules for addressing disk drives and/or naming files *may* change.

A FEW LAST WORDS ON THE QUESTION OF HARDWARE

To get properly started you will need to have an adequate set of computer hardware.

The most critical hardware item for a microcomputer database system is the disk drive system. A disk system used with a database management system should have enough storage capability to store the entire database on a single disk. (In chapter 3, we discuss how to determine the size of your database in BYTES.) The CPU can only use the data contained on the disk drives that are connected to it. That data is said to be ON-LINE. If you have floppy disk drives, only the floppy disks that are actually inserted into the disk drives are ON-LINE. If you own a computer and desire to use it for a database application you will want to carefully evaluate your disk capability.

If you have not selected a computer as yet, the most effective process for you and your bank book to follow is: select the database system, determine your storage requirements, select a computer system that (1) is compatible with your database software system and (2) that supports your storage requirements and offers a reasonable way of adding additional mass storage if it should become necessary.

What About Hardware Systems?

SECTION TWO

In Section Two we will build a more comprehensive understanding of database planning and use. We begin with the simplicity and importance of good planning and proceed to build, modify and maintain and finally use substantial databases. We build on the groundwork and examples familiar from Section One.

CHAPTER IV

PLANNING YOUR DATABASE

Planning is often considered a nuisance, particularly by the beginner. This is not limited to the database beginner. Unfortunately, if you do not plan well enough, you may be unhappy with the result and, or course, you might have to do it all over again.

Take, once again, the example of making a paper database using a typewriter. If the typist does not plan the layout of the columns properly the 'database' will, most likely, 'fall off' the right margin of the paper. This is certainly not catastrophic, but it is a nuisance, and it will have to be done over.

The same is true with our computer database. It is not going to fall off the paper, but if not properly planned, you may have to go back and do some additional work to get it the way you want it. In fact, one pretty good approach to planning your database is to take a shot at it expecting to have to redo it once or twice. This process is called ITERATIVE ENHANCEMENT. One of the benefits of working with a computer (as opposed to paper) database is that you can make really major changes to the database without having to re-enter the data. The computer, in most cases, can be used to recover most —if not all— of the data that was stored in the database before the change was made.

The first step in planning your database is to know what you want to do with it. Then you can decide what to put in it. The next step is to make a list of the items that must be included. Avoid concern over perfection. Nearly any shortcoming can be easily repaired or overcome.

As a first example, let's look again at the liquor store database created in Chapter II. This 'inventory' database is intended to tell us the stock on hand and how much it is worth. When we created this database, we just stated the column headings to establish the record struture. If we were planning this database, we would make a list of the items to be included:

> Brand of Liquor
> Size of Container
> Kind of Liquor
> Retail Price
> Wholesale Price
> Quantity on Hand

This list describes what was included in the liquor store inventory from Chapter II. Since we first set this up, we have thought of at least one additional item that should be included:

> Location of the Item

This oversight is simple to correct. We will review the necessary process step by step and you can see how easy it is to change. This should truly set your mind at ease.

You already have a database, B:INVENTRY, and it has a lot of data in it. What do you do? You need to add a field and you don't want to lose the data that you have already entered.

NO PROBLEM! You can solve this one from your keyboard in minutes without losing any data at all. Furthermore, **there is more than one solution** — more than one way to do this.

SOLUTION #1: CREATE A NEW FILE

One possible solution is to create a new file (we will call it B:NEWFILE) which has the same structure (fieldnames, fieldtypes, and widths) as B:INVENTRY but adds a new field to handle the location. We create B:NEWFILE by using the dBASE II command CREATE. Once the new file has been created, all of the information stored in B:INVENTRY is appended to the new file.

The create operation is shown in Screen 4-1. Note that we chose to place the new field LOCATION in the middle of the record. This was done to illustrate that the database management system deals with fields — the position of the field within the record is unimportant.

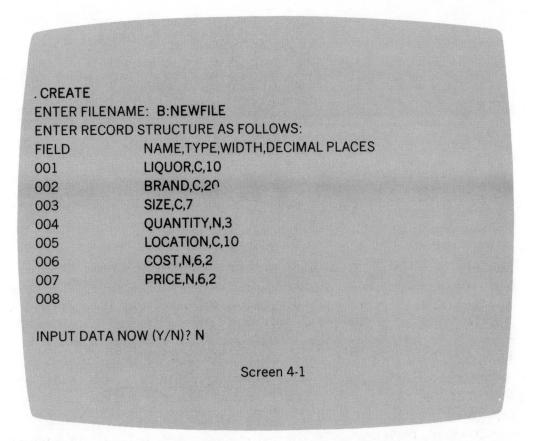

```
. CREATE
ENTER FILENAME:  B:NEWFILE
ENTER RECORD STRUCTURE AS FOLLOWS:
FIELD              NAME,TYPE,WIDTH,DECIMAL PLACES
001                LIQUOR,C,10
002                BRAND,C,20
003                SIZE,C,7
004                QUANTITY,N,3
005                LOCATION,C,10
006                COST,N,6,2
007                PRICE,N,6,2
008

INPUT DATA NOW (Y/N)? N
```

Screen 4-1

Our decision this time is NO, we don't want to input data now. Entering 'no' takes you out of the database that was just created. To work with this database again you must employ the command USE. All of the data stored in the file B:INVENTRY can be added to the file B:NEWFILE with the dialog shown in Figure 4-2.

```
. USE B:NEWFILE
. APPEND FROM B:INVENTRY
00015 RECORDS APPENDED




            Screen 4-2
```

In the abbreviated example above, a new database file was created by the CREATE process. All of the information stored in the database file B:INVENTRY is added to the new file (B:NEWFILE) by using the dBASE II command APPEND. All of the information appears in the proper fields even though the new field — LOCATION — was placed in the 'middle' of the database.

Now we have two files, B:NEWFILE and B:INVENTRY. At this point, each contains the same information. B:NEWFILE contains the added field — LOCATION. We would like to name this file B:INVENTRY. We have no use for the old B:INVENTRY. We can get rid of the old B:INVENTRY and rename B:NEWFILE as B:INVENTRY with the dialog shown in Screen 4-3.

```
. DELETE FILE B:INVENTRY
FILE HAS BEEN DELETED
. RENAME B:NEWFILE TO B:INVENTRY




            Screen 4-3
```

SOLUTION #2: MODIFY THE STRUCTURE

dBASE II allows you to change the structure of the database in a manner similar to EDIT. This is accomplished with a command MODIFY STRUCTURE. Unfortunately, when we 'edit' the structure in this way, all of the data is destroyed. To best handle this situation we can accomplish the 'editing' by making a copy of the structure and then 'editing' our copy of the structure. The original database is still intact and unchanged. We proceed with the commands as shown below in Screen 4-4.

```
. USE B.INVENTRY
. COPY STRUCTURE TO B:NEWFILE
. USE B.NEWFILE
. MODIFY STRUCTURE
MODIFY ERASES ALL DATA RECORDS ... PROCEED(Y/N) Y
```

Screen 4-4

You can now safely modify the structure of B:NEWFILE without affecting the original database B:INVENTRY. Screen 4-5 is the duplicate of our original database B:INVENTRY. Even though it looks the same as B:INVENTRY, it is really the duplicate file, B:NEWFILE. B:INVENTRY still exists — safely apart from our upcoming structure modification.

```
              NAME        TYPE      LEN       DEC
FIELD 01:LIQUOR           C         010       000       :
FIELD 02:BRAND            C         020       000       :
FIELD 03:SIZE             C         007       000       :
FIELD 04:QUANTITY         N         003       000       :
FIELD 05:COST             N         006       002       :
FIELD 06:PRICE            N         006       002       :
FIELD 07:                                               :
FIELD 08:                                               :
FIELD 09:                                               :
FIELD 10:                                               :
FIELD 11:                                               :
FIELD 12:                                               :
FIELD 13:                                               :
FIELD 14:                                               :
FIELD 15:                                               :
FIELD 16:                                               :


                         Screen 4-5
```

In this example we will insert a new field between QUANTITY and COST. To accomplish this we press the RETURN key four times. This positions the cursor at the beginning of the fieldname COST. Then,

- Press the CONTROL key and the 'N' at the same time.

This inserts a blank at field 5. Then,

- Type in the new fieldname, fieldtype, and fieldwidth.

The display will look like Screen 4-6 below.

	NAME	TYPE	LEN	DEC	
FIELD 01:	LIQUOR	C	010	000	:
FIELD 02:	BRAND	C	020	000	:
FIELD 03:	SIZE	C	007	000	:
FIELD 04:	QUANTITY	N	003	000	:
FIELD 05:	LOCATION	C	001	000	:
FIELD 06:	COST	N	006	002	:
FIELD 07:	PRICE	N	006	002	:
FIELD 08:					:
FIELD 09:					:
FIELD 10:					:
FIELD 11:					:
FIELD 12:					:
FIELD 13:					:
FIELD 14:					:
FIELD 15:					:
FIELD 16:					:

Screen 4-6

Press CONTROL W. The database B:NEWFILE now has the new field that you wanted to add. The existing data from B:INVENTRY can be added and the file can be renamed just as in the last example. (Screen 4-2 and Screen 4-3). To do so, append from B:INVENTRY:

.APPEND FROM B:INVENTRY
00015 RECORDS APPENDED

At this point you have both the new and old versions of your database. It is best to take a look at the new database to make sure that everything is okay before deleting your old version.

.LIST

When the computer's response to your request to 'list' appears on the screen, you will see an additional blank space between the columns quantity and cost. This blank space will hold the contents of the new field location. If everything looks all right, you can get rid of the old file B:INVENTRY. Simply:

```
.DELETE FILE B:INVENTRY
FILE HAS BEEN DELETED
.RENAME B:NEWFILE TO B:INVENTRY
```

This completes Solution #2: the process of modifying the structure of your database.

You see, it's a piece of cake. Nothing to it. You can put in (CREATE) whatever you want in the beginning and then ITERATIVE ENHANCEMENT will let you refine your approach as you get deeper into the task and realize things you didn't anticipate when you started.

Let's now move back a bit — back to the concept of planning before you get into CREATING and USING your database. You are ready to know more and need additional information about working characteristics and limitations of the database.

If you were to set up a database on paper using a typewriter you would need to do two things — assign column headings for each of the columns, and figure out how many spaces to use for each column. You must do both of these for a computer database. The kind of information in each column is also part of planning your computer database.

There are three kinds of fields used in computer databases. These are:

```
CHARACTER FIELDS
NUMERIC FIELDS
LOGICAL FIELDS
```

CHARACTER FIELDS are the most common kind of field. A character field may contain anything that can be printed by a typewriter. This includes letters (both upper and lower case), numbers, and special symbols such as ?,&,< etc. as well as 'space'. Normally a character field can be used for any purpose. In fact, we can make every field in the database a character field. Some typical examples of character fields are NAME, ADDRESS, and PHONE from the telephone directory example in Chapter I.

The size (width) of a character field is the number of typewriter spaces that would be required to contain the longest entry for that field. Each letter, number, special symbol, and 'space' counts as one character. Each character takes one BYTE of memory. Each time we have related the field width to space on a typewritten page we have been comparing that to the space in the computer's memory. Field width is always in BYTES. The number of bytes is the same as the number of spaces required to put the field on a typewritten page.

NUMERIC FIELDS can contain only numbers. They are normally used only when the numbers they contain may be used in arithmetic. They can contain either whole numbers (called integers) or decimal numbers. In addition to the numbers such as 1 and 8 they can contain decimal points (periods) and minus signs (—). A negative number such as —281.65, occupies 7 spaces (BYTES) and has 2 decimal places. In most database systems the positive (+) sign is understood and does not need to be entered. The minus sign and the decimal point each occupy a space and must be counted when determining the field width.

Numeric fields are also 'right justified' by the computer. Because of this, they are often used for numbers that are not to be used in arithmetic but are normally shown as right justified. Character fields are normally 'left justified' by the computer. Examples of number columns that are right and left justified are shown in Figure 4-1.

LEFT JUSTIFIED	RIGHT JUSTIFIED
1	1
10	10
100	100

Figure 4-1. Justification

LOGICAL FIELDS are used where there are only two possibilities for the data. For example, bills are either paid or they are not. Students either attended a class or they didn't. You are either reading this or you are not. Logical fields always take one BYTE (space). Data may be entered as T or F (for TRUE or FALSE), or alternatively as Y or N (for Yes or No).

Close on the heels of determining what 'type' of field you want is assigning that field a fieldname. From Chapter I we know that the fieldname must contain 10 or fewer characters. Fieldnames should be selected so that they are adequately descriptive, but as short as possible for convenience. For example, suppose you were to have fields that contained the inventory quantity for every month of the year. If you like to type you might have fieldnames like JANUARY, FEBRUARY, etc. Otherwise, JAN, FEB, etc. should do just fine.

The other 'decision option' is relevant only to numeric fields: does it contain decimal numbers and if so, how many places maximum will you allow? That decision is pretty straightforward and we will see it made as we work again through the 'plan' process — this time CREATING the structure on our screen.

We are going to work through the plan — a 'Database Plan' — for the inventory database that we created in Chapter II. This is currently B:INVENTRY, amended to add the item's location. We will use the same fieldnames, fieldtypes, and widths that we used in the example. The new field containing the item's location could be called LOCATION. It will be a character field. For the purpose of this example, we will arbitrarily assign a width of 10 to this field.

A plan for the database B:INVENTRY would look something like that shown in Figure 4-2. Notice that it resembles a database itself. If you have several databases it is often wise to have a database which contains the database plans. This database of plans could be called a DATA DICTIONARY.

FIELD DESCRIPTION	FIELDNAME	TYPE	WIDTH	DECIMALS
Kind of Liquor	LIQUOR	C	10	
Brand of Liquor	BRAND	C	20	
Size of Container	SIZE	C	7	
Retail Price	PRICE	N	6	2
Wholesale Price	COST	N	6	2
Quantity on Hand	QUANTITY	N	3	
Location of the Item	LOCATION	C	10	
TOTAL NUMBER OF BYTES			62	
EXPECTED NUMBER OF RECORDS			1000	

Figure 4-2. Sample Database Plan For B:INVENTRY

This database has seven fields and requires 62 bytes of memory for each record. Before you decide — 'big deal, why should I go through this whole process for something that I can do in my head?' — you should consider that your database could well require several dozen fields with hundreds of bytes for each record. If this should occur, then you must compare your plan with the resources available to you. Each database system as well as your computer has limitations that must be taken into account if your application becomes truly large.

Computer limitations affecting microcomputer database systems come primarily from the capacity of the disk drive(s). Consequently, they can normally be resolved by either adding additional disk drives or disk drives with significantly greater capacity.

It is encouraging to note that the size of the database is often matched by the financial resources available. Those who have very large database needs usually have resources to match. Mass storage limitations normally have hardware solutions with cost implications in the range of a few hundred to a few thousand dollars.

The limitations imposed by the database system are somewhat more interesting than the limitations of memory storage room. Database system limitations could easily lead you off on a quest for some new and wonderful database management system that will be a panacea for all your problems. The alternative to this potentially costly approach is to use your head.

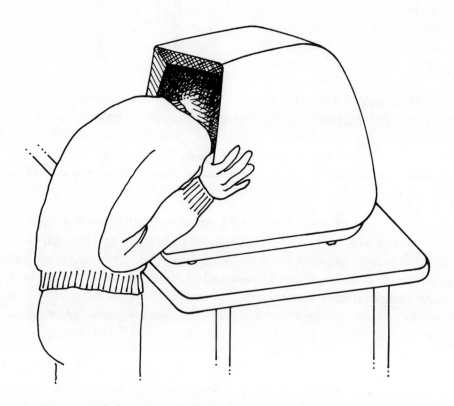

The resource limitations imposed by the database system are typically as follows:

Number of Fields
Field Width
Number of Bytes in a Record
Number of Records in a File (database)

In dBASE II, 32 fields are allowed, each field is limited to 254 bytes, and each record to 1000 bytes. The number of records is limited to 65,535. This means the maximum size for each dBASE II database file is 65,535,000 bytes. That's pretty big. It's so big that you are really unlikely to encounter the limits.

To give you an idea of just how big this is consider the following. Using a standard typewriter, 8 1/2 by 11 paper, standard 1 inch margins, and pica type, the database requires more than 18,670 pages. A microcomputer with a Winchester Disk can 'read' the database at about 16,000 characters a second. This means that it takes the computer over an hour just to 'read' the database. When you encounter databases that are this large you are likely to encounter limitations in either the computer hardware or the operating system. CP/M 2.2, a widely used microcomputer operating system, limits files to 8,000,000 bytes for example.

One of the most common problems in database planning is that a plan requires more fields than are offered by the database system. The solution to this is easy. Simply split the plan into two or more databases. When this happens, each database becomes a 'file' within a larger database and perhaps you should refer to each of the databases as a file. All of the files taken together become the database.

When you split your plan into two or more files you must find a way to link the databases together. One way to do this is to have one or more common fields in each database file. As an example, lets look at a database for an elementary school. Our hypothetical database plan might have 60 fields and look like Figure 4-3.

FIELD	FIELD DESCRIPTION	FIELDNAME	TYPE	WIDTH	DECIMALS
1	Student's Name	NAME	C	30	
2	Room Assignment	ROOM	C	3	
3	Grade	GRADE	C	1	
4	Teacher's Name	TEACHER	C	15	
5	Retained last year Y/N	RETAINED	L	1	
—	—	—	—	—	
—	—	—	—	—	
57	Home Address	ADDRESS	C	30	
58	Home Telephone Number	PHONE	C	8	
59	Emergency Notification	ENAME	C	30	
60	Emergency Telephone	EMERGENCY	C	8	
	TOTAL NUMBER OF BYTES				341
	EXPECTED NUMBER OF RECORDS				600

Figure 4-3. Elementary School Database Plan

This is a pretty good example of a nominally large database. It requires mass storage of a little over 200,000 bytes (characters). It is said that more than 90% of all databases have less than 100,000 bytes. This illustrates something even large operations with professional staffs often overlook.

YOU SHOULD UNDERSTAND YOUR APPLICATION BEFORE YOU BUY YOUR HARDWARE AND SOFTWARE.

For this application, the minimum hardware configuration should include two disk drives where at least one of the drives is capable of storing about 500,000 bytes. You can get by with less, but you may be constrained within the range of things you may want to do. For example, if you should want to add a field to a database you will need 400,000 bytes to store the two databases at the point where you have appended all of the records from one database to the other.

The only database software limitation (for dBASE II) in this example involves the number of necessary fields: there are more fields than one database file can support (32). The solution is to break the database into two or more files. When databases are broken and occupy 2 or more files, we must link the files together. This is done using a 'common element' — some piece of data that appears consistently across the whole database, like the student's name.

There is nothing novel about this. It is quite likely that each student's file (for regular paper files) is on more than one piece of paper. In a paper file, the student's name would commonly appear on each piece of paper. In our database, each file has a NAME field which contains the student's name. The total number of fields is now 61 and the total number of characters is 371. There are 61 fields because we have added 'NAME' again in field 33 to identify who information in 34 — 60 belongs to. This installs the necessary common element after 34 — 60 is split off from the first database.

The only problem arises where there are two students in the school with the same name. This is not altogether unlikely. We minimize this problem by making three fields — NAME, ROOM & GRADE — common to both files. The plan now requires 63 fields with 375 bytes per 'record.' Using dBASE II, our plan can be implemented with 2 files which form the complete database.

Another possible solution is to assign each student an identification number. This has some merit. It requires fewer bytes than the recommended

80

solution and requires only two additional fields instead of three. On the negative side, it might require additional effort on someone's part to insure that the identification number is unique for each student.

Let's take a look at the fields ROOM, GRADE, and TEACHER. In many areas of this country that would be redundant information. In an elementary school, Mr. Jones would normally be uniquely assigned to room 201 and grade 6. If this is the case, it is reasonable and efficient to establish a third database file which contains information regarding the teachers. Since it is likely that the school would have a file on personnel information anyway, this allows the elimination of a field from the student file. In this particular case that saves approximately 9000 bytes of memory (600 records x 15 bytes) — plus the bother of typing the 600 names in the first place, and changing it all when a teacher is replaced.

This school database now has three files. The files are related to one another. This is, by the way, the true definition of a RELATIONAL database system. Files may be related to each other and needless duplication minimized. As a matter of fact, the technical term for a database file is RELATION. It is usually wise to group information that is used together into a single relation. This is because it is simpler to work with one database than with two or more.

In our example, the three database files (Relations) are linked as shown in Figure 4-4. This Figure illustrates the way in which the files can be tied together.

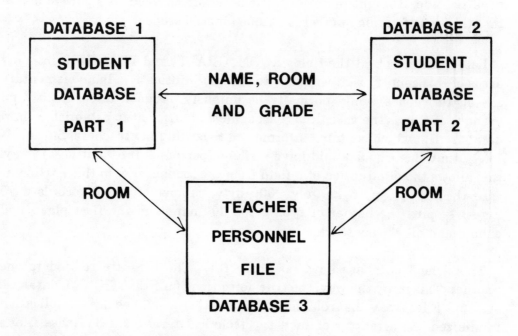

Figure 4-4

One other item to consider in planning is described by Figure 4-5.

NAME	LAST NAME
	FIRST NAME
	MIDDLE INITIAL
ADDRESS	NUMBER
	STREET
	CITY
	STATE
	ZIP
	COUNTRY
TELEPHONE	AREA CODE
	NUMBER

Figure 4-5. Two Possible Sets Of Fields

This Figure has a particular point: an item can cover a lot of ground. In one case we have three fields, in the second, eleven. Your application will likely be something in the middle. To decide whether to combine data items into a single field or not requires an understanding of how the data will be used. One rule of thumb is if the items are rarely, if ever, used separately, they may be combined. Grouping items such as last name, first name, and middle initial into a single name field often allows for more efficient use of space. And it's certainly simpler to do.

The list in Figure 4-5 covers exactly the same information that we covered in the original telephone directory example. There is, however, information here that was left out of the original: the area code and zip code. These two items could be covered in the address and phone fields of the original example. In the second example of fields, you would most likely add a field for the zip code. Whether or not you add a field for area code or include it as a part of the phone number will probably depend on how you intend to use the information.

As your database gets larger, it takes more time for the computer to search through it. If the database is small, you need not be careful at all regarding the space assigned to a field. If it is large, however, you may very well want to carefully consider the size of each field — and even if you should have the field at all.

Remember: although we used the number of typewriter spaces to illustrate the number of bytes used in a field — a typewritten page will contain many blank spaces used to separate the columns.

DO NOT DO THIS IN A DATABASE

Unused bytes are not needed to 'separate' the fields. If the field contains a student's age, and the maximum possible age is 9, use only one byte for that field. Separating the fields when they are displayed, either on the terminal or on a printer, is a separate issue that is covered in a later chapter.

As we mentioned at the beginning, planning is often considered a nuisance. The urge to get started is sometimes overwhelming. As you gain experience, you will also gain an appreciation of the immense value of thorough planning. Planning forces you to think the problem through before you act. If it seems like a nuisance, remember that no planning will likely result in the larger nuisance of having to do the work over again. Think of planning in terms of iterative enhancement (i.e. improvement through repeated attempts).

1. Begin with a workable 'skeleton' of the plan.

2. Build on this workable framework until you have the system ready to put on the computer.

The most serious trap you can get caught in is to seek perfection. This can be prohibitively expensive and may hinder your success in achieving a viable database plan. Avoid doing this.

Remember, you may be unfamiliar with computer database management systems, but the concept, construction, and use of computer databases is definitely not difficult. There are a lot of parallel examples from the pencil and paper world that you are familiar with. Relax and make the necessary connections from your pool of experience. A computer database is an easy step to take into your future. Not to say, at all, that it's trivial — just easy.

CHAPTER V

BUILDING YOUR DATABASE

When you have finished the planning process, you are ready to 'begin construction' of your database. This construction phase begins by creating the structure (framework) for the database, which we discussed in depth in Chapter IV. It is completed by entering all of the data — a record at a time into this structure. The most serious problem you are likely to encounter during this data entry period is to keep from being bored to death.

Building Your Database

Prior to the development of microcomputers and database management systems, the process of creating a file wasn't as easy. It was a lengthy and expensive process involving expensive hardware and the use of professional programmers. Of course, you could have learned to program yourself, but until recently there wasn't any way to avoid the use of expensive hardware. Today, with one of the available database management systems and inexpensive microcomputer hardware you can easily do this yourself. And, unless you are a very slow typist, it can be done quickly.

SOME REVIEW FROM CHAPTER I

The process of data entry was illustrated in Chapter I by the construction of two sample databases, B:FONEBOOK and B:INVENTRY. In these examples, we learned that the mechanical process of creating the database structure is in two parts.

FIRST, select a FILENAME (title) for the database.

SECOND, define each of the FIELDS (columns) in the database.

The rules for selecting a FILENAME are determined by the computer's operating system. Different microcomputers may use different operating systems. Hence, the particular rules for selecting filenames may vary from computer to computer. Since the examples in this book use CP/M® — a widely used operating system — all filename activity is discussed in terms of CP/M® rules. If you have, or are considering, a computer which does not use CP/M® you should consult the computer's instruction manual for its filename rules.

A CP/M® filename may have eight or fewer letters and numbers. It must begin with a letter. It may not contain blank spaces. Some examples of valid filenames are:

CHAPTER1
SCHOOL
FONEBOOK

Examples of INVALID filenames are:

CHAPTER 1	Too long and contains a blank space
GOBBLEDEGOOK	Too long
8CHAPT	Starts with a number

The purpose of the filename is to identify to the computer which file you want to work with. If the computer has more than one disk drive, you must also normally add a disk drive identifier in front of the filename. In CP/M®, disk drives are identified by a letter followed by a colon (e.g. A:). The valid filenames from above could be identified as:

A:CHAPTER1	File is on the 'A' drive
C:SCHOOL	File is on the 'C' drive
B:FONEBOOK	File is on the 'B' drive

The disk drive identifier is not a permanent part of the filename. It will vary depending upon which disk drive the disk is inserted in. For example, if we remove the disk containing the file CHAPTER1 from drive A and insert it into drive B, the file will be identified as B:CHAPTER1.

You may have more than one database file with the same name as long as the files are not on the same disk. The system will not permit you to have two database files with the same name on a disk.

A database is a particular kind of FILE, a '.DBF' file. There are other kinds of files the computer may work with. In Chapter I, we worked briefly with another kind of file, called a FORM file, ('.FRM' file) which we used to prepare the liquor store inventory example report. A database file and a form file may be on the same disk and have the same filename. When a database file is created, dBASE II automatically appends '.DBF' to the filename. When a report is created '.FRM' is automatically added to the filename. '.DBF' and '.FRM' are examples of filetypes. The filename is determined by you, the user. In dBASE II, the filetype is determined by the system. The filetype is important to the system which uses the information in the performance of its tasks.

Once you have selected a filename for your database, you are ready to define the database structure. The information that the computer needs is:

(1) How many FIELDS (columns) are there.

(2) The name of each column.

(3) The width of each column (e.g. number of characters or digits).

(4) The kind of information in each column (e.g. numbers, characters, or logical).

The database management system will prompt (ask) you for each item it needs as it needs it. An example of the dialog that created the database B:INVENTRY is shown as Screen 5-1.

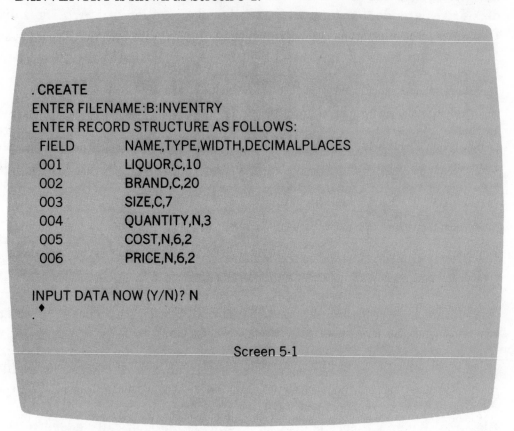

```
. CREATE
ENTER FILENAME:B:INVENTRY
ENTER RECORD STRUCTURE AS FOLLOWS:
  FIELD         NAME,TYPE,WIDTH,DECIMALPLACES
  001           LIQUOR,C,10
  002           BRAND,C,20
  003           SIZE,C,7
  004           QUANTITY,N,3
  005           COST,N,6,2
  006           PRICE,N,6,2

INPUT DATA NOW (Y/N)? N
  ♦
  .
```

Screen 5-1

We have created a database whose filename is INVENTRY and which is located on disk drive B. A rough analogy to what we have done to this point is to take a new manila folder, write 'INVENTORY' on the tab, type column headings on a blank paper, draw lines on the page separating the colunns, place the paper in the manila folder, and then place the manila folder in a file cabinet.

SAME PROCESS: SOME NEW VARIABLES

As you enter the information shown in Screen 5-1, it is possible you might make a typing error. As an example, let's suppose that we had misspelled the entry SIZE in field 3. If we notice the error before we have moved to field 4 we can correct it. On most keyboards is a key which is labeled RUB or DEL. Pressing this key will erase the character to the left of the cursor and move the cursor one character space left. The typographical error can be corrected by erasing all of the entry up to the point of the error and then retyping the entry from that point.

Suppose you notice an error after you have moved to another field — you can't back up to fix it. Continue to define the remaining fields. Press the N key when asked if you want to enter data.

Type in MODIFY STRUCTURE following the dot prompt. A display which is similar to Screen 5-2 will appear on your terminal. The error can be corrected by moving the cursor down to the incorrect field, typing in the correct information, and then CONTROL W. (W for 'write' — tells the computer, 'Exit from edit, write what I've done to the disk.')

	NAME	TYPE	LEN	DEC	
FIELD 01:	LIQUOR	C	010	000	:
FIELD 02:	BRAND	C	020	000	:
FIELD 03:	SIZE	C	007	000	:
FIELD 04:	QUANTITY	N	003	000	:
FIELD 05:	COST	N	006	002	:
FIELD 06:	PRICE	N	006	002	:
FIELD 07:					:
FIELD 08:					:
FIELD 09:					:
FIELD 10:					:
FIELD 11:					:
FIELD 12:					:
FIELD 13:					:
FIELD 14:					:
FIELD 15:					:
FIELD 16:					:

Screen 5-2

To begin entering data into your new database, you must first open the file. In dBASE II, this is accomplished with the USE command. In our example this would be:

. USE B:INVENTRY

The data entry process is initiated by the command APPEND.

. APPEND

```
RECORD # 00001

LIQUOR        :              :
BRAND         :                        :
SIZE          :        :
QUANTITY      :    :
COST          :    :
PRICE         :    :


                    Screen 5-3
```

The computer will begin prompting you to enter the data for the first record as shown in Screen 5-3. The APPEND command actually adds records to the end of the database. If there were already 49 records in the database, the response to an APPEND command would be identical to Screen 5-3 except that the record number would be 00050.

When you have entered all of the data for a record, as shown in Screen 5-4,

```
RECORD # 00001

LIQUOR        :SCOTCH      :
BRAND         :AULD COUNTRY            :
SIZE          :QUART:
QUANTITY      : 23:
COST          : 5.59:
PRICE         : 9.31:


                    Screen 5-4
```

the computer will automatically clear the screen and begin prompting you to enter data for the following record.

ON ENTERING DATA

The value of the database depends, in large part, upon quality. It is of little solace to tell the tax auditor, 'I know there are some errors, but it was really fast!' Because data entry is often dull and repetitious work, it is tempting, in fact it is common practice, to turn this part of the process over to the lowest paid help available. This is a **BAD** idea.

In many cases, there will be an enormous amount of data to enter into the new database. Most real liquor stores, for example, have far more than 15 items in stock. Data entry will be, far and away, the most time consuming part of most database usage. Entry is done at human speed; retrieval is done at computer speed.

In addition, it is the part of the process most prone to error. Entering a single record, or even several, can be accomplished without error. It is unlikely that error free input can be extended to hundreds and, perhaps, thousands of records.

ERRORS WHILE ENTERING DATA

When you are adding a large number of new records to the database, such as during the initial construction, it is likely that something will happen to cause you to lose track of where you are. Or, as you are busily working, it may dawn on you that you made an error during data entry on the last record. You cannot simply 'back up' to change what is wrong. You must get out of APPEND. This is accomplished by pressing the return key at the very beginning of the first field. If the record you are working in when you realize your error is essentially correct, go ahead and finish it and exit from append at the beginning of the next record entry prompt. If the record you are working in is really a mess, you can escape by pressing CONTROL Q which not only gets you out of the APPEND mode, but erases the erroneous record you've created, as well.

Once you have exited from the APPEND process you may look at the last record by using either DISPLAY or EDIT A. Either will display the last record you had entered. EDIT A presents the data in exactly the same form as did APPEND. EDIT A also allows you to correct any errors in the RECORD.

In order to actually correct errors, we need to understand cursor movement. You have to be able to position the computer at the location of the error before you can correct it.

Errors can be easily corrected by moving the cursor back to where the error is and typing in the correct information. On many terminals there are four keys with arrow symbols on them. These keys should allow you to move the cursor while entering data into the database. The 'up' and 'down' arrows should move the cursor a field backward and forward in the record. The 'right' and 'left' arrows should move the cursor one character space to the right and to the left.

Some terminals may either not have cursor control keys or the keys may not work with the database system. If this is the case, you will have to use the control key + either E, S, D or X to move the cursor. You will remember our discussion from Chapter 1 about the CONTROL (CTRL) key: it permits most of the letter keys to have a 'third meaning.'

In dBASE II this third meaning is used to provide for cursor control and other aids for editing data — as will now be explained.

The cursor is moved about with the help of the CONTROL key. The symbol ^ indicates the CONTROL key. ^D means press the CONTROL key down and hold it down while you strike the D key. This action will, in dBASE II, cause the cursor to move one space to the right. Similarly, ^S will move the cursor one space to the left. ^E moves the cursor one field backwards toward the beginning of the record. ^X moves the cursor forward one field. The CONTROL key, together with the E,S,D, and X keys can be used to move the cursor around so that you can correct errors or just change the entry as needed.

Now that you know how to move the cursor, you can correct the mistakes you have made. Remember, EDIT A will get you back into previously entered records and allow you to make corrections. Control W will 'write' those corrections to the disk.

Error correction can actually be even simpler if you notice the error in time. The computer is very tolerant of bad typing, getting mixed up, whatever goof you can do — up to the point where the data is permanently stored. This permanent storage does not occur until you exit from a record and enter another. The exit process fixes the information. Until then, nothing in that record is permanently stored. So, you can move around and change at will, AS LONG AS YOU ARE STILL IN THE RECORD. It is therefore advisable to make a quick visual check of your entries before going on to the next record.

Let's go through some sample corrections. Suppose that you have typed in TESSTT and you wanted TEST. The final T can be removed by placing the cursor on the last T and striking the space bar. The surplus S can be removed in two ways; place the cursor on the second S and either press the RUB (or DEL key), or use CONTROL G (^G). Rub eliminates the character (and the space that it occupied) to the left of the cursor. Similarly, Control G eliminates the character that the cursor is on. In both cases the result is TEST.

Of course, you could have just typed over the word TEST and used the space bar to clean up the extra two characters at the end. Regular keyboard characters can be printed on the screen wherever the cursor is located. It doesn't matter whether or not there were characters there already. The last character entered 'wins'.

The other side of removing characters is adding characters. Suppose that you had typed TET when you wanted TEST. You want to insert the letter S between the E and the T. This can be accomplished by placing the cursor on the last T. To insert the letter S press ^V, type S, and then ^V again.

^V is the 'insert' command. ^V is also what's called a 'toggle' command. You're undoubtedly familiar with toggle switches which are either 'ON' or 'OFF.' A toggle command is similar in that it represents a status of something that is either 'ON' or 'OFF.' The same ^V turns it ON and OFF. If it is ON and you type ^V it will be OFF, and vice versa. While it is ON, you may insert as many characters as necessary. It will be ON until you ^V, turn it OFF.

There is another element in data entry — besides error correction — which may concern you. Perhaps you have available only part of the information necessary to complete a record, but you still want to enter what you have.

If you are only going to enter a part of the information for a record, enter the information and then press ^C. This will advance you to the next record immediately without needing to step through each of the remaining fields.

In the past few paragraphs, we have noted several helpful CONTROL KEY functions (^G=delete character; ^V=insert; ^Q=get rid of data from this record I've made a mess of so I can start over).

There are many other aids available to you by way of the CONTROL key. The examples given in these paragraphs should serve to acquaint you with the general idea as well as the basic services.

To this point, the process of constructing a database has been purely mechanical. You create a file structure according to simple rules and then you enter data. Data entry continues until all of the data has been entered. At this point the database is ready to be used to fulfill some purpose — such as providing you with the information needed to help manage a business.

If the data entry job is small, the simple mechanical approach described above is probably the 'best' way to get the job done. It is straightforward and simple.

If there is a lot of data to enter, it might be a good idea to consider finding ways that the computer system can actually help with the entry process.

COMPUTER DATA ENTRY ASSISTANCE

There are some built in data entry aids as well as some simple procedures that you can write which enable the computer to assist or perform some of your data entry tasks for you. In the remaining pages of this chapter, we will discuss 3 such processes:

1. CUSTOM PROMPTS
2. SET CARRY ON/OFF
3. MENU SYSTEMS

CUSTOM PROMPTS and MENU SYSTEMS are developed by simple procedures which you will learn to write to suit your needs. A 'procedure' is an easy way of getting the computer to perform special things for you. The details of 'teaching' the computer a procedure will be discussed in part 4 which begins with Chapter XI. The use of the procedure generated end products — custom prompts and menu systems — is included here because of their great added value to the data entry process. 'SET CARRY ON/OFF' is a 'built-in' aid, initiated by a simple command.

CUSTOM PROMPTS

CUSTOM PROMPTS illustrate one kind of assistance the computer can provide. In our liquor store example, the fieldnames are reasonably descriptive of the field contents. This is often — but not always — the case. When it is not the case, then it would be nice to be able to include more information. For example, we could make the prompt read something like:

ENTER THE KIND OF LIQUOR (SCOTCH, WHISKEY, ETC) :

This is much more descriptive than simply displaying the word LIQUOR. In general, this sort of help from the computer is very desirable. It is particularly helpful if you have a lot of data and want someone to help you enter it. This is especially true if the filenames are not particularly descriptive of their intended contents.

As we mentioned before, custom prompts such as this one can be provided with relative ease via PROCEDURES.

Procedures, like databases, have filenames. In dBASE II, procedures are called COMMAND files. The same filename rules that apply to other files apply to COMMAND files. You must also identify which disk drive the procedure is stored on.

To show you how a CUSTOM PROMPT might work, we will assume that a procedure to provide descriptive prompts has been written. We will call our sample procedure B:ENTRY. To have the computer do the procedure in dBASE II, you enter

. DO B:ENTRY

following a dot prompt. DO:B:ENTRY works just like APPEND. APPEND would bring up an empty 'standard' record form; B:ENTRY brings up an empty 'customized' record form. DO B:ENTRY produces Screen 5-5.

```
RECORD # 00001

ENTER THE KIND OF LIQUOR (VODKA, GIN, ETC.)     :           :
ENTER THE BRAND NAME                            :                    :
ENTER THE CONTAINER SIZE (CASE, QUART, ETC.)    :        :
QUANTITY OF THIS SIZE AND BRAND                 :    :
WHOLESALE COST                  :           :
RETAIL PRICE                :       :


                        Screen 5-5
```

Incidentally — a passing comment — writing procedures for database management systems is not at all hard. In fact, it can be fun as well as rewarding.

SET CARRY ON/OFF

We'll take a short break from what you can teach the computer to do and talk about another capability it has on its own.

In many databases, there is often a lot of redundant data to be entered. In a school, there are far more children than there are rooms and teachers. In our liquor store example, there are several brand names for each kind of liquor. In many cases, the data may be grouped in such a way as to reduce the amount of data that must be typed in. In the liquor store, the stock on the shelves is grouped by kind of liquor — Vodka, Bourbon, etc — for the convenience of the customer. The various sizes for a given brand are usually grouped within the brand.

When redundancy is grouped, as in these two examples, the computer can reduce the amount of typing required by 'carrying' the data forward from record to record. In dBASE II, this capability is 'turned on' by the command SET CARRY ON. It is turned off by SET CARRY OFF.

Let's consider how data entry would progress for our example if CARRY were SET ON. First, with APPEND, we get an initial screen display and enter the Record 00001 data.

```
RECORD # 00001

LIQUOR        :SCOTCH       :
BRAND         :AULD COUNTRY          :
SIZE          :QUART:
QUANTITY      : 23:
COST          : 5.59:
PRICE         : 9.31:


                    Screen 5-4
```

Normally, then, the prompt display would appear, blank, headed by RECORD ˆ 00002. With CARRY ON, the display is exactly like Screen 5-4 with the record number advanced to 00002. All we need do is change those fields which are different from Record 1. When we advance, the record 3 display will be exactly as record 2 at the time of the advance. This particular assistance can accomplish 2 things; it can reduce the amount of typing, and it can reduce the number of errors due to typing.

A MENU SYSTEM

Now back to another technique you can 'teach' the computer to do. With this technique, a procedure is written that provides the data entry person with a set of 'multiple choices' to select from. This technique is called a MENU SYSTEM. It minimizes the possibility of typing error.

Unfortunately, it increases the possibility of absolute error. It is profitably used where the data to be input has little in common from record to record and, consequently, the idea of carry forward is of no value.

Let's suppose that we have written a procedure to do a liquor store inventory using the MENU technique. In our hypothetical example, the terminal might provide the display shown in Screen 5-6.

```
                    SELECT FROM THE FOLLOWING

        A — HALF PINT              1 — SCOTCH
        B — PINT                   2 — BOURBON
        C — FIFTH                  3 — GIN
        D — QUART                  4 — WHISKEY
        E — LITER                  5 — VODKA
        F — 1/2 GALLON             6 — IRISH WHISKEY
        G — 2 LITER                7 — RUM
        H — GALLON                 8 — BRANDY
        I — CASE                   9 — OTHER


ENTER SIZE SELECTION FROM THE LEFT COLUMN   :  :

ENTER TYPE OF LIQUOR SELECTION FROM THE RIGHT COLUMN   :  :

ENTER BRAND NAME   :                          :

ENTER QUANTITY   :  :

ENTER RETAIL PRICE   :    :

ENTER WHOLESALE COST   :  :


                        Screen 5-6
```

This particular example uses some of the helpful aspects of our earlier discussion of custom prompts, as well as the menu selection idea. The information 'gallon of gin' is entered as H3.

In this example, the entire data entry and menu process is accomplished with one screen display. If the data to be entered is more extensive we might require more than one screen display. For example, if there are 30 or 40 choices for each of the liquor and size 'selections' we might want to use one screen display for each of the two selection columns. This would have lead directly to three successive screen displays for this menu example.

Menu procedures as well as other elaborate prompt systems can be profitably used when you need a lot of data entered and don't want to have to explain either the nature of the data or anything about the database system. There are cases where everything that needs to be entered can be menu selectable.

CONDITIONAL REPLACEMENT

In addition to these three rather straightforward data entry aids, there is another, somewhat sneakier method available for entering certain kinds of "conditional" information.

The example appropriate to this CONDITIONAL REPLACEMENT method comes from a student database built for an elementary school.

The database contains the NAME,ROOM,GRADE, and TEACHER for each student. When the database is 'built' only the NAME, ROOM, and GRADE need to be entered. When this is completed for each child, the TEACHER information can be added with an operation like the dBASE II command REPLACE.

```
.REPLACE TEACHER WITH 'MR. JOHNSON' FOR ROOM='101'
.REPLACE TEACHER WITH 'MRS. ADAMS' FOR ROOM='201'
ETC
```

The best thing about the process of building a database is that, usually, it is a one time operation. This process — entering the data — is sometimes called LOADING the database. The 'build' process is critical to all future use of the database. If the information is not complete or if it is entered with errors, the ultimate results will be incomplete and erroneous. And you will be unhappy. Once the data has been correctly entered you can begin to make profitable use of it — which is what this is all about.

The options you have when 'building' the original data base range from the simple and straightforward APPEND, to increasingly elaborate procedures for more descriptive prompts. Other aids that can be used to minimize your effort are:

- carry data forward from record to record,
- MENU selection, and
- CONDITIONAL REPLACEMENT.

These aids reduce the amount of typing required. The larger and more complicated your database, the more likely the procedure idea is to be of value to you.

CHAPTER VI

MODIFYING AND MAINTAINING YOUR DATABASE

Once the database has been built it is inevitable that it will be changed. All kinds of change necessitate record changes. In addition to internal record change, in fields like QUANTITY and PRICE, some records must be added and some deleted. Evolving government regulations may require new fields be added to the database. This major everyday activity — changing the database — is called UPDATING.

Updating is the database activity certain to consume the most time. This is mostly due to the fact that it is a manual operation. Routine reports and other output products are usually accomplished automatically at computer speeds and require relatively little time.

The frequency with which the database is updated will depend, in large part, on your needs. Ordinarily, there are updating tasks which must be done daily. Others are suitable to update weekly, monthly, and so on. Other updating tasks are done only as specifically needed.

Our Little Liquor Store, for example, might update an inventory database as each new shipment is received. Employee hours, depending upon the situation, might be updated either daily or weekly. The magnitude of the updating tasks will, of course, depend upon the particular application.

Change normally falls into one or more of three categories;

(1) Changing the Database Structure
(2) Adding and Deleting Records
(3) Changing the Content of Records

CHANGING THE STRUCTURE OF THE DATABASE

Generally, the structure of the database is not often changed. Structural change is normally in response to a change in the business environment — such as a new government regulation. Because of possible data loss consequences, great care should be taken whenever the structure is altered.

Whenever the structure of the database is changed (in dBASE II this is called MODIFYING) the contents of the database will be damaged. To protect against this, a copy of the database must be made whenever the database structure is changed. Once this copy is made, the structure can safely be modified.

An example of this process in the dBASE II system is shown in Screen 6-1.

```
.USE B:INVENTRY
.COPY ALL TO B:NEWFILE
00015 RECORDS COPIED
.MODIFY STRUCTURE
MODIFY ERASES ALL DATA RECORDS ... PROCEED? (Y/N) Y


                        Screen 6-1
```

Changes that may be made to the structure include:

> Adding Fields
> Deleting Fields
> Changing the Name of a Field (special operation)
> Changing the Size of a Field
> Changing the fieldtype

The computer will display the database structure on the terminal as shown in Screen 6-2.

```
              NAME        TYPE    LEN     DEC
FIELD 01:LIQUOR           C       010     000      :
FIELD 02:BRAND            C       020     000      :
FIELD 03:SIZE             C       007     000      :
FIELD 04:QUANTITY         N       003     000      :
FIELD 05:COST             N       006     002      :
FIELD 06:PRICE            N       006     002      :
FIELD 07:                                          :
FIELD 08:                                          :
FIELD 09:                                          :
FIELD 10:                                          :
FIELD 11:                                          :
FIELD 12:                                          :
FIELD 13:                                          :
FIELD 14:                                          :
FIELD 15:                                          :
FIELD 16:                                          :


              Screen 6-2
```

In this mode you are able to move the cursor about on the screen in order to effect the desired changes. The cursor may be moved using the cursor control keys. If your keyboard does not have these keys, the cursor can be moved by using the control keys as shown in Figure 6-1. A field can be deleted by positioning the cursor on the fieldname and pressing either CONTROL Y or CONTROL T. A field can be added by positioning the cursor to the desired location of the new field and pressing CONTROL N. This will move all of the following fields down one position and display a blank field at the position of the new field. Type in the FIELDNAME, FIELDTYPE, and WIDTH to complete adding the field. Existing fields can be modified by positioning the cursor to the field to be modified and typing the new information in over the old information. Typing CONTROL W tells the computer that you have completed modifying the structure. Control Q aborts the change.

CONTROL KEY	EFFECT
S	Moves cursor 1 character left
D	Moves cursor 1 character right
E	Moves cursor 1 field back
X	Moves cursor 1 field forward
T	Deletes field
Y	Erases entry
N	Inserts blank field space at cursor location
W	Save new file structure
Q	Abort the change operation

Figure 6-1. Control Key Functions For MODIFY STRUCTURE

At this point you have a copy of the old database and a new database which has no records. The data from the old database that belongs in the new one is LOADED (RELOADED) into the new database by the dBASE II command APPEND.

.APPEND FROM B:NEWFILE
00015 RECORDS APPENDED

The contents of all fields that are common to both the new and the old databases will be added to the new. New fields will be blank. A field which has been made smaller will truncate the data when it is added to the new database. Character fields will lose their rightmost characters while number fields will lose their leftmost digits. A problem arises when a fieldname has been changed. In this case the computer will assume that this field is a new field and that the old one is deleted. Therefore this field will be blank in the new record.

Changing the fieldname requires a special operation. One way to accomplish that is to unload and reload the database. When this approach is used, fields should not be added or deleted. All fieldwidths should also remain unchanged. In dBASE II this operation can be accomplished with a variation of the COPY command. (In some systems this is called UNLOADING, which is a special kind of copying. The 'unloaded' database cannot be directly used by the database management system. This special copy is used to reload the database system once the structural changes have been made.)

. COPY ALL TO B:NEWFILE SDF

This stores the contents of the database into NEWFILE in a very special way. There are no fields any longer — although the data is an array of rows and columns. It cannot be used directly by the database management system. It can however, be used by a word processing system. SDF stands for System Data Format. This is an example of an UNLOADED database.

The unloaded data that is temporarily stored in the field B:NEWFILE can be loaded into the database INVENTRY by

. APPEND FROM B:NEWFILE SDF

If the structure of INVENTRY is the same as it was before except that a fieldname was changed — the database is now restored to its original condition — with the new fieldname.

It is reasonable to expect that the structure of the database will not be changed often. When it is undertaken, it is wise to make an extra copy — just in case something goes wrong. This is one case where the penalty for error is extreme.

ADDING AND DELETING RECORDS

A far more common change operation involves adding records to or deleting records from the database. New employees are hired, others quit or retire. These operations are ordinarily quite straightforward.

The process of adding a record to the database has been described in Chapter II and V. In dBASE II, this is the APPEND process. Whenever a record is appended, it is placed at the end of the database. In dBASE II the end of the database is called the bottom. There are occasional circumstances where it is desireable to insert a record into the middle of the database. In dBASE II, this is accomplished by the command INSERT. This command is similar to APPEND except that it adds the new record wherever you desire in the database. To use this command you must first position yourself in the database. This is accomplished with the GOTO command.

. GOTO RECORD 127

The use of INSERT will now insert a blank record at record location 128. All of the records that were after record 127 will be renumbered and moved down one record position. The old Record 128 becomes Record 129, the old

Record 129 becomes Record 130, and so on. Once this re-ordering has been completed, the screen will be erased and the blank Record 128 will be presented for data entry exactly as in append.

Records are removed by a two step process. First, a record is marked for deletion. Examples of commands which mark a record for deletion are:

.DELETE RECORD 216

.DELETE FOR NAME='BRONCO, BILLY'

.DELETE FOR LIQUOR='IRISH MALT' .AND. BRAND='KILARNY GREEN'

Each time there is a delete command, the computer should respond with the number of records that have been deleted. This allows you to take corrective action and 'undelete' those records that were inadvertently deleted. The dBASE II command to 'undelete' records is RECALL. Examples of RECALL are:

.RECALL ALL

.RECALL RECORD 216

.RECALL FOR NAME='BRONCO, BILLY'

The actual removal of the record(s) is done with a second command. In dBASE II, that command is PACK. PACK will permanently remove those records you have marked for such removal by DELETE.

If the database is used in conjunction with tables such as dBASE II INDEX files, the database may require re-indexing whenever records are added or removed. Some relational database management systems may allow adding or removing records while an index file is in use. When this is the case, the index file is automatically updated when each record is added or removed. This is normally the case with the Hierarchical and Network (CODASYL) database systems.

When a record is appended while an index file is in use, the record will appear to be inserted into the database. If, for example, the database is indexed on NAME the records will appear to be in alphabetical order. A new record will appear to be placed in its proper alphabetical location. It is actually added to the end of the database just as it is without an index file.

CHANGING RECORD CONTENTS

There are several ways that you can change the contents of data fields. When you are making specific changes to individual records — such as entering the number of hours an employee worked on Monday — they are best changed one at a time with a full screen operation such as dBASE II's EDIT command. The EDIT command presents the same display as the APPEND command.

EDIT is the only command which requires a knowledge of the Record number. Let's suppose that we want to edit the liquor store inventory record for quarts of Auld Country Scotch. If we happen to know that the record number for this item is Record 1 we can start the edit process with:

.EDIT 1

The CRT terminal will present the display shown in Screen 6-3. The record can be changed by moving the cursor to the desired field and typing in the new information. The cursor can be moved with the cursor control keys. If there are no cursor control keys the cursor may be moved by use of the CONTROL key as shown in Figure 6-2.

To illustrate the EDIT capability we will change the QUANTITY from 23 to 33, the COST to 5.75, and the PRICE to 10.98. This is accomplished by the following sequence. Hold down the CONTROL key. While it is held down press the X three times. This moves the cursor from LIQUOR field to the QUANTITY field. Type in 33 and a RETURN. This replaces the value 23 with 33 and moves the cursor to the COST field. Type in 5.75 and a RETURN. This replaces the value of 5.59 with 5.75 and moves the cursor to the PRICE field. Type in 10.98 and a RETURN. This replaces the value 9.31 with 10.98 and advances to the next record — in this case Record 2. Press CONTROL R. This will select the previous record — Record 1. The record will appear as shown by Screen 6-4.

```
RECORD # 00001

LIQUOR        :SCOTCH       :
BRAND         :AULD COUNTRY              :
SIZE          :QUART:
QUANTITY      : 23:
COST          :  5.59:
PRICE         :  9.31:


                           Screen 6-3
```

Adjacent records may be selected by ˆR (the previous record) and ˆC (the following record). The operation may be aborted by using ˆQ. Aborting the changes can be quite convenient if you find that you have, for some reason, been editing the wrong record. The changes may be permanently incorporated by any of ˆW, ˆR, or ˆC. The EDIT command will allow you to step through the database one record at a time by repeated use of ˆC.

CONTROL KEY	EFFECT
S	Moves cursor 1 character left
D	Moves cursor 1 character right
E	Moves cursor 1 field back
X	Moves cursor 1 field forward
Y	Erases field contents
U	Toggle — deletes/undeletes record
V	Toggle — turns character insert mode on/off
W	Save new file information
Q	Abort the change operation
R	Edits previous record
C	Advances EDIT to next record

Figure 6-2. Control Key Functions For EDIT

```
RECORD # 00001

LIQUOR        :SCOTCH      :
BRAND         :AULD COUNTRY            :
SIZE          :QUART:
QUANTITY      : 33:
COST          :  5.75:
PRICE         : 10.98:


                              Screen 6-4
```

If it should happen—as is almost always the case—you don't know the record number, it can be acquired in a number of ways, such as:

.DISPLAY FOR LIQUOR='SCOTCH'.AND.BRAND='AULD COUNTRY'

.LOCATE FOR LIQUOR='SCOTCH'.AND.BRAND='AULD COUNTRY'.AND
.SIZE='QUART'

Each of these will provide the desired record number. The second command example also 'positions' the database to the desired record. In this case the record can be edited by EDIT A. EDIT A will edit the current record.

Another approach which allows you to see and change the contents of the database is illustrated by the dBASE II command BROWSE. A graphic description of BROWSE is provided by cutting a square section from a piece of paper. Now place the paper with the hole cut in it over another paper that has writing on it. You have a sort of window opening onto the second page. By moving the window about you can view the entire contents of the second page a little at a time. BROWSE is a window onto the database that allows you to view a section of the database at a time and make changes wherever you desire. The difference between browse and edit functions is that browse will show part of several records on the screen at a time while edit will show all of one record.

The browse and edit commands are necessarily limited to manual operation. In addition, only one record can be changed at a time.

The database system must also provide for changing several records at once because a CONDITION has changed. One example of this occurs when a school teacher leaves and is replaced by a new teacher. Using EDIT or BROWSE would require typing the new teacher's name for each record being changed. An easier approach for this situation is to use the dBASE II command REPLACE. If the new teacher is Mrs. Jones and the old teacher is Mr. Smith and the room number is 21, the command can be either of those shown below. When REPLACE is used for a condition, every record that meets the condition will be changed.

.REPLACE TEACHER WITH 'MRS. JONES' FOR ROOM='21'

.REPLACE TEACHER WITH 'MRS. JONES' FOR TEACHER='MR. SMITH'

Database applications that require frequent changing can benefit from the kinds of procedures illustrated in the last chapter: descriptive prompts and MENU's. The use of procedures can be an effective substitute for your memory. They also allow the database to be manipulated by less skilled (hence less costly) help. As in the last chapter, the two techniques can be combined to provide every powerful and versatile aids to changing the database.

Screen 6-5 illustrates the operation of changing an elementary school database using a PROCEDURE. The procedure demonstrated uses a combination of descriptive prompts and menus to help the person entering the data. The particular example will add records, delete records, and provide the capability of changing records. The records contain the NAME, ROOM, GRADE, TEACHER and fields containing other information about each student.

```
                SELECT ONE OF THE FOLLOWING:

        A — ADD A NEW STUDENT

        C — CHANGE A STUDENT'S RECORD

        S — CHANGE THE NEXT STUDENT'S RECORD

        D — ERASE A STUDENT'S RECORD

        Q — END THE COMPUTER SESSION

    PLEASE ENTER YOUR SELECTION   :   :

                    Screen 6-5
```

If selection C is chosen, the computer will provide a new display. This new display is depicted by Screen 6-6.

```
        PLEASE ENTER THE FOLLOWING INFORMATION

    PLEASE ENTER THE STUDENT'S GRADE   :   :

    ENTER THE STUDENT'S ROOM NUMBER   :         :

    ENTER THE STUDENT'S LAST NAME   :                   :

    ENTER THE STUDENT'S FIRST NAME   :                 :

                    Screen 6-6
```

When the information above has been provided to the computer there is a short display while the computer locates the student of interest. The computer will then display the student's record as in Screen 6-7.

```
                    STUDENT RECORD

   STUDENT'S NAME (LAST NAME FIRST):JEFFERSON, THOMAS:

   ROOM :201:      GRADE:5:      TEACHER'S NAME :JOHNSON:

   BIRTHDATE (MONTH/DAY/YEAR):11/27/71:

   .....and so on for the rest of the student record.

                      Screen 6-7
```

The information to be changed is selected by moving the cursor to the field to be changed and typing in the new information. When the changes have been completed, the operator is returned to the first (main) menu. A new change operation is selected and the process is repeated. The menu option A would go directly to the student record. The student record — when displayed would, of course, be all blank. Menu option S provides a means of moving from record to record, as when entering test scores, without the necessity of entering information unnecessary for the purpose. Menu option D would use the second display — requesting information about the student. When the delete option has been selected the procedure should always provide a second chance for the operator. After the information has been entered, the computer should provide the operator a display like that in Screen 6-8.

```
                    DELETED RECORD

        YOU HAVE DELETED THE FOLLOWING STUDENT

                  JEFFERSON, THOMAS

            GRADE 5       ROOM 201

   ARE YOU SURE THAT YOU WANT TO DELETE THIS STUDENT (Y/N):   :

                    Screen 6-8
```

This example is representative of the use of menus and descriptive prompts as an aid to the person who must enter new information into the computer. It is somewhat analogous to the use of paper FORMS by clerical help. When this was the case, there was a written procedure that told the clerk which form to use. In the case of the computer, the procedure tells the computer which 'form' to use. If the operator using the computer is not familiar with the computer the procedure should contain at least one menu selection for 'operator assistance' or HELP.

One of the additional values of the procedure is to formalize the process of changing the database. This can be accomplished while minimizing the effort required by the operator. If the data entry process can be made interesting, if not entertaining, the likelihood of error is reduced. For most database applications it is imperative that the database not contain errors. Some menu operations minimize the effort required and minimize the chance of spelling errors (remember here that while you might know that scocth means scotch — the computer doesn't). The opportunity exists however, for the entry of GIN instead of SCOTCH. The procedure can provide safeguards against these possibilities, however, that does require additional effort on the part of the person writing the procedure.

The last item to be covered in this chapter is the subject of maintaining the database. In this case 'maintaining' can be defined as 'safeguarding' the database. If you have a 'database' which consists of a bunch of records on paper, you are subject to some problems in safeguarding the paper records. Coffee can be spilled on part of the record, a single piece of paper can be inadvertently thrown away. However, few things short of absolute calamity (fire, flood, hurricane, etc.) are catastrophic to the 'database'. This is not true with a computer database. A computer database might be contained on a thin sheet of magnetized mylar. A finger inadvertently placed on the mylar film can damage the stored information. A cigarette will destroy it completely. One piece of film is more vulnerable than a filing cabinet full of paper. All of the things that work to make the database convenient to use also work to make it susceptible to disaster.

Much of the foregoing gloom can be avoided by adhering strictly to some simple procedures. A back-up copy or two of the database should be maintained and protected. This is one very good reason for having at least two disk drives on your computer system. If you have more than two disk drives you can make the copy easily by placing a fresh disk in one of the additional drives and using the copy command. If your database is located on the B disk drive and the fresh disk has been placed in the C drive, the copy can be made by:

. COPY ALL TO C:BACKUP

If you have only two disk drives, your database is located on the B disk drive, and there is enough space available on the A drive to contain the database the copy can be made by:

. COPY ALL TO A:BACKUP

If you have only two disk drives, your database is located on the B disk drive and there is insufficient space available on the A drive to contain the database use the dBASE II command QUIT. QUIT will return you to your computer's operating system.

. QUIT

*** END RUN   DBASE II ***

A> ◆

If drive A has a copy of CP/M, your operating system, the following procedure will provide you with a backup copy of your database. Remove your database disk from the B disk drive. Insert a fresh disk into the B drive. Type ^C. Type the letters PIP after the A>. The computer will respond with a '*' on the line below the A>. Remove the disk from drive A. Place the database disk in drive A. Type B:=*.*[V]. This will copy and verify all of the contents of disk drive A to disk drive B. Remove the database disk and the backup copy. Replace the original A disk in the A drive. Replace the original database disk into the B drive. Press the RETURN key. This entire process is shown on Screen 6-9.

```
. QUIT

*** END RUN        DBASE II ***

                  · · · · · · · · · · · · (remove database disk from B)
                  · · · · · · · · · · · (insert back-up disk into B)

A>  ^C

A> PIP

                  · · · · · · · · · · · (remove CP/M disk from A)
                  · · · · · · · · · · · (insert database disk into A)

*B:=*.*[V]
*

                  · · · · · · · · · · · (remove database disk from A)
                  · · · · · · · · · · · (insert CP/M disk into A)

A>  ^C

A>  ♦

                  · · · · · · · · · · · (you now have a backup disk in B)
```

Screen 6-9

One approach to back-up of your files is to have two copies. The two copies are used on alternate days. The concept of using two back-up copies will work to your ultimate advantage. Properly followed, this protects against loss of all except, perhaps, one days work. If you can limit the liability to this value (with the exception of absolute disaster; fire, etc.) you have done about as well as you can do. It's actually possible to protect against major disasters to a higher degree than is possible with paper records. It is not reasonable to maintain two sets of paper records in two separate locations. This is not unreasonable with the computer database however. Since you can copy the database onto floppy disks or tape, the copy(s) can easily be stored at a remote location — providing some reasonable protection for disasters short of war.

Modifying and Maintaining
Your Database

CHAPTER VII

USING YOUR DATABASE

There are really two parts to using the database. The first, keeping it current (updating), was covered in the last chapter. The second, getting it to do something for you is the subject of this chapter.

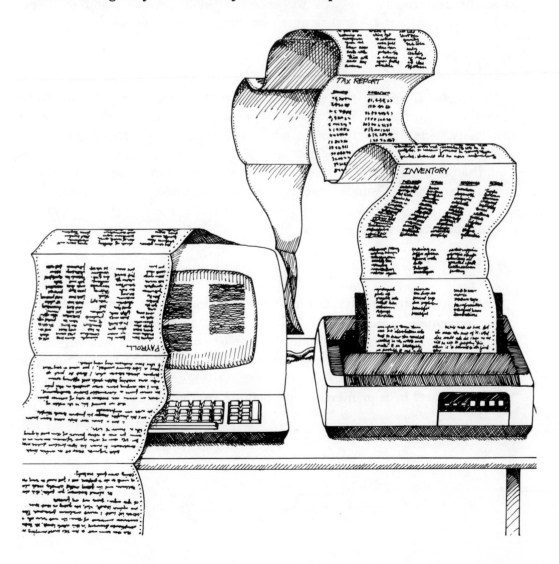

TWO BASIC USES OF THE DATABASE

There are two basic database uses:

1. To perform standard services i.e., generate payroll reports, tax reports, current inventory, etc.

2. To obtain specific information whenever necessary.

Our database management system, dBASE II, has a report writer suitable for producing a variety of standard reports. You may also write 'procedures' that allow you to produce specialized, custom reports suited to your own very specific needs. Specific information necessary to a 'non-routine' process is obtained from the computer keyboard using a 'query language.' We will first discuss 'reports,' which we encountered briefly in Chapter II, and follow later in the chapter with query languages and processes.

REPORT

In Chapter I, we used the liquor store inventory example to introduce the report writing concept. Most modern database systems provide a capability for easily generating reports based on the contents of the database. The report's standard capabilities can be exploited from the keyboard, providing you, the user, with information extracted from the database. In Chapter II, we learned that a simple dialog with the computer sets up a reporting process the computer can remember. We can use this report over and over again. The process is initiated by

.REPORT

The ensuing dialog with the computer is reproduced from Chapter I for your convenience in Screen 7-1. In this version of Screen 7-1, however, additional comments are inserted in lower case letters. The report the operator prepares, based on the database B:INVENTRY, from the report form filled out in Screen 7-1, is shown as Figure 7-1. If you want the resulting report to be printed by your printer, the command is

.REPORT TO PRINT

ENTER REPORT FORM NAME: B:INVENTRY
ENTER OPTIONS, M=LEFT MARGIN, L=LINES/PAGE, W=PAGE WIDTH
PAGE HEADING? (Y/N) Y
ENTER PAGE HEADING: LIQUORSTOREINVENTORY
DOUBLE SPACE REPORT? (Y/N) N
TOTALS REQUIRED IN REPORT? Y
SUBTOTALS IN REPORT? (Y/N) Y
ENTER SUBTOTALS FIELD: LIQUOR   *(subtotals for each liquor)*
SUMMARY REPORT ONLY? (Y/N) N   *(allows the indiv. entries)*
EJECT PAGE AFTER SUBTOTALS? (Y/N) N
ENTER SUBTOTAL HEADING:
COL   WIDTH,CONTENTS
001   20,BRAND   *(no. of spaces, fieldname)*
ENTER HEADING: BRAND
002   7,SIZE
ENTER HEADING:
003   3,QUANTITY
ENTER HEADING: QTY
ARE TOTALS REQUIRED? (Y/N) Y
004   6,COST
ENTER HEADING: COST
ARE TOTALS REQUIRED? (Y/N) N   *(remember * means multiply)*
005   7,COST*QUANTITY   *(cost times quantity)*
ENTER HEADING: INVEST
ARE TOTALS REQUIRED? (Y/N) Y
006

Screen 7-1

Using Your Database

```
PAGE NO. 00001
09/15/81


                    LIQUOR STORE INVENTORY

         BRAND                    QTY    COST    INVEST
```

BRAND		QTY	COST	INVEST
* SCOTCH				
AULD COUNTRY	QUART	23	5.59	128.57
AULD COUNTRY	1/2 LIT	7	9.78	68.46
AULD COUNTRY	PINT	88	2.74	241.12
** SUBTOTAL **		118		438.15
* VODKA				
REAL RUSSIAN	QUART	35	3.78	132.30
REAL RUSSIAN	1/2 LIT	9	7.95	71.55
REAL RUSSIAN	PINT	75	1.49	111.75
** SUBTOTAL **		119		315.60
* WHISKEY				
SOUTHERN RYE	QUART	32	5.11	163.52
OLD WYOMING	PINT	44	1.98	87.12
OLD WYOMING	QUART	19	5.29	100.51
THE NEW SOUTH	QUART	4	7.49	29.96
** SUBTOTAL **		99		381.11
* BOURBON				
SOUTHERN ARISTOCRACY	PINT	5	0.99	4.95
SOUTHERN ARISTOCRACY	FIFTH	22	1.78	39.16
SOUTHERN ARISTOCRACY	QUART	21	3.50	73.50
SOUTHERN ARISTOCRACY	1/2 GAL	3	6.89	20.67
SOUTHERN ARISTOCRACY	1/2 LIT	5	6.47	32.35
** SUBTOTAL **		56		170.63
** TOTAL **		392		1305.49

Figure 7-1. Computer Report On Liquor Store Inventory

This report works well because liquor 'kinds' are grouped together in the database. If they were not grouped, the result would be a shambles. If we are unsure whether or not the liquors are blocked, we should first index the database to group the data — ensuring a coherent report.

.INDEX ON LIQUOR TO B:LIQUOR
.USE B:INVENTRY INDEX B:LIQUOR

One report prompt which we answered 'no' to in Screen 7-1 was 'SUMMARY REPORT ONLY.' With, instead, a 'yes' to this prompt, we get a different report than the one shown in Figure 7-1. Such a summary report is shown below in Figure 7-2. Note there is no information in the cost column. The only values printed are the category subtotals.

PAGE NO. 00001
09/15/81

LIQUOR STORE INVENTORY

BRAND	QTY	COST	INVEST
* SCOTCH	118		438.15
* VODKA	119		315.60
* WHISKEY	99		381.11
* BOURBON	56		170.63
** TOTAL **	392		1305.49

Figure 7-2. Computer Prepared Summary Of Liquor Store Inventory

The lack of information in the cost column results directly from our 'no' to the prompt 'SUBTOTALS IN REPORT?'

Using the original example, we request a detailed report on Bourbon:

.REPORT FOR LIQUOR='BOURBON'

This provides the report presented as Figure 7-3. This particular report gives 'Bourbon only' information. Since the database is so small, the example result is valuable only as an illustration. It shows the ability to 'report' on any identifiable subset of the database. This capability is invaluable if the database is large. If it is large, you might first obtain a printout on only the summary. Subsequent reports, such as Figure 7-3, are selected based on information in the summary.

PAGE NO. 00001
09/15/81

LIQUOR STORE INVENTORY

BRAND		QTY	COST	INVEST
* BOURBON				
SOUTHERN ARISTOCRACY	PINT	5	0.99	4.95
SOUTHERN ARISTOCRACY	FIFTH	22	1.78	39.16
SOUTHERN ARISTOCRACY	QUART	21	3.50	73.50
SOUTHERN ARISTOCRACY	1/2 GAL	3	6.89	20.67
SOUTHERN ARISTOCRACY	1/2 LIT	5	6.47	32.35
** SUBTOTAL **				
		56		170.63
** TOTAL **				
		392		1305.49

Figure 7-3. Computer Prepared Report For Bourbons Contained In The Liquor Store Inventory

If we want an even quicker, if somewhat less elegant response we can use two Query Language Processor commands. We will discuss query languages and processes in a moment, but include this example here to show side by side results of the two major ways you go about 'using' your database. This process of QLP commands and responses is shown in Screen 7-4.

```
.DISPLAY OFF BRAND,QUANTITY,COST,COST*QUANTITY FOR
LIQUOR='BOURBON'

SOUTHERN ARISTOCRACY      PINT       5      0.99      4.95
SOUTHERN ARISTOCRACY      FIFTH     22      1.78     39.16
SOUTHERN ARISTOCRACY      QUART     21      3.50     73.50
SOUTHERN ARISTOCRACY      1/2 GAL    3      6.89     20.67
SOUTHERN ARISTOCRACY      1/2 LIT    5      6.47     32.35

.SUM QUANTITY,COST*QUANTITY
                                   392              1305.49
```

Screen 7-4

You can see from our rather extensive use of the liquor store inventory example that extracting information from a database via report is really very simple. For a business environment, it would be easy as well as pertinent to develop many special applications reports from your database. These might include accounts payable, accounts receivable, payroll, personnel, or etc. in addition to an inventory system such as ours for the liquor store. There is great value in keeping a database as the foundation for all these applications activities. Each separate application is easily accommodated with its own custom procedure or report. At the same time, however, everything originates in a common database — a common pool of information that can be accessed for specific, non-routine tasks in addition to the standard structure you have up and running on its own regular cycle.

An example. Suppose a company is considering a new union contract. Management would like to know the impact of the contract before agreeing to the terms. If, as is often the case even in large, professionally designed and managed systems, the personnel and payroll systems are separate, it might take considerable effort, if it's even possible, to determine the impact of the proposed contract. When they are in fact separate systems, there is much duplication of effort — and information. For example, a computer system for doing payroll will need the employees name, employee number, number of dependents, salary rate, etc. A computer personnel system needs similar information. When the systems are separate, the information that is stored by one cannot always be used by another.

On the other hand, if personnel and payroll systems use a database system, the information might be available directly from the keyboard with a simple query.

This 'separateness' of often necessarily related information is one of the things that led to development of databases. In a database, unlike in an 'accounts payable program,' or etc., as far as the computer is concerned, the stored information is independent of the application. It is up to the user to impose the application they want to see when requesting use of the database. This brings us to something mentioned a couple times recently: information available by query.

EXTRACTING INFORMATION (QUERY)

Database systems respond to user requests for information (queries). The part of the database system that does this is called the QUERY LANGUAGE PROCESSOR (QLP). dBASE II's query language processor is called APPLICATIONS DEVELOPMENT LANGUAGE (ADL).

You use the QUERY LANGUAGE to tell the computer what to do. Most contemporary QUERY LANGUAGES are very much like ordinary English. In some systems, the only function of the QLP is to extract information from the database. In this case, it is said that the QLP is a 'READ — ONLY' function. In dBASE II, ADL is also used to UPDATE the database. This means it can 'WRITE' as well as 'READ.'

QUERY LANGUAGES

There are two kinds of Query Languages: Procedural and Non-Procedural.

- Procedural is the traditional computer language. With this language, you tell the computer, step by step, what you want it to do to produce your desired result. Examples of procedural languages are BASIC, FORTRAN, PL/1 and COBOL. In all of these, you tell the computer how to find an answer — not what the problem is.

126

- Non-Procedural language allows you to state the problem and the computer figures out how to get the answer.

From the personal telephone book example, if you want to know how many of the entries are in Glendale,

.COUNT FOR'Glendale'$ADDRESS

is an example of a non-procedural command. Here you have told the computer what you want and it figures out how to do it.

Some query languages have features of both. dBASE II's ADL is both a procedural and non-procedural query language. Procedural and non-procedural features of relational database system query languages are sometimes referred to in technical terms:

- Procedural features are called the RELATIONAL ALGEBRA.
- Non-procedural are called the RELATIONAL CALCULUS.

It isn't clear that these terms have any particular value other than to attempt to intimidate the non-professional.

Specific information necessary for a non-routine process is obtained from the computer keyboard using the Query Language. If the database has a lot of fields, you may need to keep and use a data dictionary (Chapter III) for this purpose. To make use of the database — under any conditions — you must know the FIELDNAMES and what is contained in the FIELDS.

A Query Language that allows you to make very high level requests from the keyboard has three parts to a command. These are:

- the NAME,
- the SCOPE, and
- the CONDITION.

The command 'NAME' is normally representative of the function required. dBASE II examples of command names are DISPLAY, SUM, COUNT, LOCATE, and LIST. Scope determines how much of the database the command applies to. Condition means that the command applies if the database record meets the condition stated. Examples of possible requests are:

. SUM QUANTITY FOR LIQUOR='BOURBON'

. COUNT FOR 'Robert'$NAME

. DISPLAY QUANTITY FOR LIQUOR='SCOTCH' .AND. SIZE='FIFTH'

. DISPLAY QUANTITY,BRAND FOR LIQUOR='SCOTCH' .AND. SIZE='FIFTH'

In the first of the four examples above, the command means 'tell us how many bottles of bourbon we have'. Specifically, it means 'add the contents of the field QUANTITY whenever the contents of the field LIQUOR are 'BOURBON.' If we omit QUANTITY from the command, it has no meaning. You cannot present the computer with a non-specific command. If you do, the result will likely be meaningless. In a good Query Language, if you do attempt this, the computer will reject the command.

In the second example, the command means 'count the records that contain the name Robert'. The third sample request asks to display the quantity (only) for each kind of fifth of scotch. In the fourth, the brand name is also displayed.

In each of these, the command is remarkably like ordinary English. This is partly because we have given each field a good descriptive fieldname.

In ADL, the entire record is normally displayed by the command DISPLAY. If less than that is desired, entering a list of fieldnames separated by commas (as in the fourth example) tells the computer to display only the fields listed.

The fourth example uses the word AND in a somewhat odd manner. Here we have said to the computer — if the contents of the field LIQUOR is 'SCOTCH' and contents of the field SIZE is 'FIFTH' display the brand and its quantity. This request will extract exactly what we want.

Suppose that we enter this request:

.DISPLAY FOR LIQUOR='SCOTCH' .AND. LIQUOR='BOURBON'

We want the computer to display all the records where the LIQUOR is SCOTCH and where the LIQUOR is BOURBON. The computer's response to the command is a dot prompt. There is no display. This means that it found none. How can this be? We know that there are entries for both bourbon and scotch, and yet the computer says there are none. This answer of 'none' actually does make sense; there is no record where the liquor is both scotch and bourbon. If we rewrite the English sentence as follows: 'We want the computer to display all of the records where the kind of liquor is either scotch or bourbon' — we get the idea. We think of the entire database when we ask for information. The computer works with one record at a time. Rewriting the command as:

.DISPLAY FOR LIQUOR='SCOTCH' .OR. LIQUOR='BOURBON'

we will get the desired result.

BOOLEAN OPERATORS

The AND and the OR are called BOOLEAN operators. The BOOLEAN operators are often called LOGICAL operators. As we have seen, .AND. and .OR. are almost the same as AND and OR in everyday English. When using these 'operators' they are written with the periods at each end to distinguish them from their ordinary English counterparts. You must be careful or you can get a strange result. It is of no small importance that you expend some effort to insure that you understand the logical operators. Otherwise you can get a TECHNICALLY CORRECT but none-the-less WRONG answer. This is where the computer does exactly what you tell it to do — not what you wanted it to do. Another boolean operator used in dBASE II is .NOT. which is described further in Chapter X.

A BIT MORE ON QUERIES

Queries are appropriate to a wide range of user needs. We might want — for one reason or another — to manipulate data contained in a database, but not actually change the data in the 'official' database. We already encountered an example of this, when we 'copied' a database so that the structure could be modified. Part of a database can be 'copied' to a new database for any desired purpose.

Let's make a copy of that part of B:INVENTRY containing only the fields BRAND, SIZE, and PRICE. To further constrain this new database, we will copy only for the 'scotch.' This operation is accomplished with a single command.

.COPY FIELD BRAND,SIZE,PRICE TO B:SCOTCH FOR LIQUOR='SCOTCH'

This produces your 'Scotch only' database. To digress briefly into specialist terminology, this copy operation is called 'the projection of the relation B:INVENTRY onto B:SCOTCH as restricted by the predicate LIQUOR='SCOTCH' '. Would you recognize that as a description of our little copying operation?

Or, let's think of another 'random' need. Say we're desperate to know what item the liquor store has the most of and what item it has the least of. We can do this either by sorting or indexing. An index provides a list of the records ordered by quantity.

.INDEX ON QUANTITY TO B:QTY
00015 RECORDS INDEXED
.USE B:INVENTRY INDEX B:QTY

To go to the beginning of the indexed database, use the dBASE II command GO TOP. To go to the end of the database use GO BOTTOM.

```
.GO TOP
.DISPLAY OFF BRAND,SIZE,QUANTITY
SOUTHERN ARISTOCRACY          1/2 GAL          3
.GO BOTTOM
.DISPLAY OFF BRAND,SIZE,QUANTITY
AULD COUNTRY                  PINT             88
```

From the keyboard we have in a straightforward manner answered our question. The item we have least of is half gallons of Southern Aristocracy and the one we have most of is pints of Auld Country.

These query examples are a tiny random sampling of kinds of things you can ask your database. The possibilities are really unlimited. The important thing is the concept and understanding enough about the process to make query use sensible and usable in light of your own needs.

YOUR OWN ELECTRONIC SCRATCHPAD

There is another very useful activity available to you: a kind of accessory to all the larger things possible with your database and computer.

Data from a single field in a record can be brought, for your convenience, into a special space in the computer's main memory. You can also, for your convenience, have the computer store a keyboard entry in its main memory. It's very much like having an electronic 'scratchpad' available to use.

A microcomputer database system provides this capability in its Query Language Processor. This temporary storage capability is convenient when performing manual operations from the keyboard. It is invaluable when writing procedures for automatic operations.

The scratchpad works a lot like the memory system in an electronic calculator. In dBASE II you are allowed to have:

- 64 separate items stored in this scratchpad memory at any one time.

- a maximum number of 254 bytes (characters or numeric digits) allowed for any one item

- total bytes allowed for all 64 items is 1536 bytes.

Each item stored in memory is a MEMORY VARIABLE. When an item (MEMORY VARIABLE) is stored into memory it must be given a name. Naming the memory variable makes it convenient for us to use and keep track of it. Each system uses some key word to tell the computer to accept an item as a memory variable. In dBASE II, this key word is STORE.

To illustrate how this 'scratchpad' memory works we will store the number 6 into a memory variable that we name EXAMPLE.

.STORE 6 to EXAMPLE

Remember:

- Within limits, you can store 64 separate items in memory at any one time.

131

- Each time you store an item, give it a name.

- If you assign the same name to two different items, only the second entry will be stored.

- To change what is stored in a memory variable, just store the new item to the old name, i.e., .STORE 7 TO EXAMPLE will put a 7 in EXAMPLE instead of the 6 we started with above.

- You cannot have 2 items with the same name at the same time.

Memory variables can be character strings, numbers, or logical data.

```
STORE 'ALPHABET' TO SOUP
```

```
STORE T TO ANSWER
```

You are allowed to use the memory for nearly any purpose. You can combine character strings into a sentence:

```
STORE 'ALPHABET' TO A
```

```
STORE ' SOUP' TO B
```

```
STORE A+B TO SOUP
```

To 'see' what is contained in a memory variable, after the dot prompt, use a question mark followed by the name of the item.

```
.? SOUP
  ALPHABET SOUP
```

Memory variables can be used to perform arithmetic.

```
. STORE 6 TO X
6
. STORE 7 TO Y
7
. STORE X+Y TO Z
13
. STORE Y—X TO W
1
    . STORE X*Y TO Z          (remember * means multiply)
42
    . STORE X/Y TO D          (the / indicates division)
0                             (here we have an example of the perversity
                               of computers. To get the decimals
                               displayed we must tell the computer how
                               many we want.)
.STOREX*1.0/Y TO D
0.8
.STORE X*1.000/Y TO D
    0.857                     (get the idea?)
```

To give you a better idea of the scratchpad memory's usefulness, let's look at the computerized check book. We enter the following field information: NUMBER, PAID TO, AMOUNT, CANCELED, and DEPOSIT. To determine the balance in the account we make the following keyboard entries:

```
. SUM AMOUNT FOR DEPOSIT TO DEP
17434.53
. SUM AMOUNT FOR .NOT.DEPOSIT TO SPENT
15997.18
. STORE DEP—SPENT TO BALANCE
1437.35
```

Here we have obtained a useful result, the current account balance, directly from the keyboard with three inquiries. To check up on the bank by checking the computer accounts against the bank's monthly statement we have:

```
. SUM AMOUNT FOR DEPOSIT.AND.CANCEL TO BANKDEP
16621.21
. SUM AMOUNT FOR .NOT.DEPOSIT.AND.CANCEL TO CANCELED
15793.23
. STORE BANKDEP—CANCELED to BANKBAL
827.98
```

Thus — with only three instructions to the computer — we have another useful result — a check on the bank's assessment of our account balance. The last result can be compared against the bank statement.

In the last two examples, we could have obtained the sums as requested without storing them. Then we could have calculated the result with a pencil and paper or a hand calculator. That would have introduced a chance for error — the hand copying of the numbers. The 'scratchpad' memory gives us direct use of the computer to perform operations using data from the database. If the data in the database is correct the chance of error is nearly zero.

In the event you get the feeling that all this is just too easy — that you must be overlooking something vital — please rest assured: it really is easy.

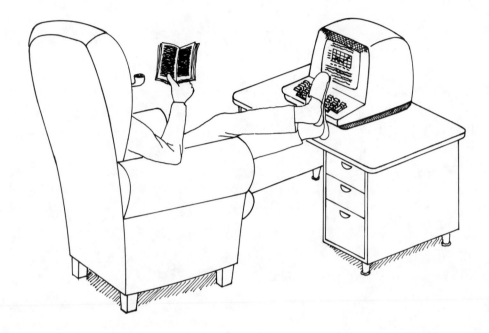

Much of today's literature on computers contributes substantially to the notion that computers should be difficult. Textbooks address the subject from a technical person's frame of reference. In such a textbook, discussion of an example command containing the .OR. would be considerably different than our discussion. The computer generated display in response to some such example command might be described in a textbook as 'the relation B:INVENTRY restricted by the predicate LIQUOR='SCOTCH' .OR. LIQUOR='BOURBON' '. A predicate, in case you simply must know, is a 'relationship among the values of the domains.'

There are times when it may seem as though professionals use specialized 'jargon' in order to justify their positions and salaries. This really isn't true. The jargon allows specialists to communicate better among themselves.

But, put the barrier that such technical language creates for someone unfamiliar with the 'computer profession' together with the general sense that computers are strange, inaccessible, difficult, or etc. and you have a good part of the reason a lot of people are haunted by 'it just can't be this easy.' In reality, most of the difficulty is simple unfamiliarity. Computers aren't just for 'computer professionals.' They have incredible capabilities that are easily accessible to anyone with a need for their capacity to store and disseminate information.

The database stores data. The DBMS allows you to extract information from that data. If we have a liquor store, we can easily learn we are dangerously low on tequila and scandalously overstocked on scotch. If we combine the sample inventory database with a database which records the stock received, we can determine annual sales of each kind and size of liquor. Over a period of time, we can learn to more efficiently manage the stock. This, in turn, results in a more efficient use of money and hence a better return on our investment. There are, of course, many other uses for database management systems in business, education and government. The point is this: it is easy to develop and effectively use this tool. It can provide real support for whatever your endeavor. It can be fun. It can release you to do more interesting kinds of activities. It may broaden your perspective, enabling you to see your entire operation from one source.

Using Your Database

SECTION THREE

Section Three discusses various types of databases, examining the nature of each system and recognizing the differences among them. In Chapter X we discuss computer logic which may seem at first glance a potentially complicated or difficult topic.

Technical and complex terminology sometimes makes computers seem mysterious and/or difficult. This impression is inaccurate and misleading — computers are really very understandable and a lot of fun besides. Section Three attempts to fill in some of the gaps and answer some common questions people ask about computers. This will hopefully increase our understanding of the computer world and allow us to make further progress with our computer databases.

CHAPTER VIII

THINGS YOU MIGHT
WANT TO KNOW ABOUT

There are a number of questions often asked about microcomputer database systems. In this and the following chapters we will attempt to answer some of the most common questions. What is an assembly language system? What is a hierarchical database? What is a Network database? What is CODASYL? What are . . . . . . ???

ASSEMBLY LANGUAGE is the computer's 'native' language. Often mistakenly called 'machine language', it is the 'language' the computer uses internally. Beyond assembly language are 'higher order languages' such as FORTRAN, COBOL, PASCAL, and dBASE II's APPLICATION DEVELOPMENT LANGUAGE (ADL). Each command or instruction in these languages is 'built' out of many assembly language instructions.

When the computer executes a command such as DISPLAY, it is actually executing a large number of assembly language instructions. Very high level languages such as BASIC and ADL use an average of 50 to 100 assembly language instructions for each high level language instruction. An assembly language database management system is one that has been 'built' out of many assembly language instructions.

Many commercial software packages are written in a high level language such as PASCAL or BASIC. This is done because it is normally easier to write the package in a high level language and because it is 'portable.' Portability means that the same package can be easily adapted for use on different kinds of microcomputers.

An assembly language program is only usable on one kind of microcomputer. To be used on other kinds of computers, it must be specifically rewritten for each kind of computer. It is often assumed that an

Assembly Language Program makes more efficient use of the machine's resources than a higher order language program such as BASIC. This is probably true if you are comparing a well written assembly language program with a well written program in a higher order language.

Since, however, it is difficult to judge whether or not two systems are equally well written, this shouldn't be a consideration in selecting a commercial system. There are advantages to each approach for a software system. Since you will almost never see a vendor advertising his system as 'mediocre' or 'average to good', you should probably discount how well written a program might be as a factor in your selection. What is really important to you: will it do your job?

SEQUENTIAL AND RANDOM ACCESS

A set of terms that is often found in articles on databases and occasionally in advertisements, is SEQUENTIAL ACCESS and RANDOM ACCESS. These terms refer to the way that the computer gets to the data. Sequential access means that the computer starts with the first record and goes through the entire database file in sequence until it finds the record that you want. Query language commands such as DISPLAY and LOCATE use a sequential approach.

.DISPLAY FOR NAME='BYERS, ROBERT'

.LOCATE FOR NAME='BYERS, ROBERT'

When DISPLAY is used in this way, the computer will examine every record in the database — starting with record 1 — in order of their record numbers (sequentially). When LOCATE is used, the computer will examine each record in the database — starting with record 1, proceeding sequentially until it comes to the record containing BYERS, ROBERT in the NAME field. This is sequential access for a particular record. Note: the time it takes the computer to find a particular record depends on where the record is in the database. If the database is large and the desired record is near the end it could take several seconds for the computer to find the record. If the computer can 'read' the entire database in one minute the average access time will be 30 seconds.

The term RANDOM ACCESS is somewhat misleading. It does not mean that the computer leafs through the database in a haphazard manner until it finds the desired record. It really means that the computer has 'direct" access to every record in the database. The word random really comes from the concept that if you choose any record at random the computer can get to that record as quickly as to any other.

A rough example of a paper database that is designed for random (direct) access is the telephone book. The telephone directory is printed in alphabetical order. When you are looking for a particular person's telephone number you use the alphabetical nature of the book to find the person's name and hence the number you desire. If you were to attempt to find the number by sequential access you would begin with the first name in the directory and go through it name by name until you find the name you desire. Sequential access is simple, reliable, and relatively slow. Direct (random) access can provide a much quicker method of getting to a particular record.

PRIMARY AND SECONDARY KEYS

If the computer is to have random (direct) access to a particular record, it needs a little help. The specific 'help' usually given the computer is a special 'PRIMARY KEY', tacked on the front of the record by the computer. The computer uses this KEY to go directly to the record, either keeping track of or calculating exactly where the record is on the disk. Then when the record is requested, the computer goes directly to the record's physical location and reads it into main memory. The 'key' information is added by the computer when the record is created. In dBASE II, the RECORD NUMBER is the 'primary key' added by the computer. If you know a record number, you can go directly to that record. Locating a record by 'key' is very fast, but it restricts the user who must first know the 'KEY'. In the case of dBASE II, knowing the 'key' means knowing the RECORD NUMBER.

The primary key must be unique. It is not likely that you can remember the primary key for each record in a computer database. That may be possible if the database is very small, however if it is that small, direct access isn't necessary.

A SECONDARY KEY is the solution to the problem of how to make the primary key useful. The database can normally have one or more secondary keys. Computer used 'keys' are generally not useful to us and 'keys' meaningful to us are generally not useful to the computer trying to gain direct access. Secondary key (s) provide the link.

Secondary keys do not provide true direct access, but they come close. Access is much faster than the average access time for sequential access. Tables provide 'translation' between secondary and primary keys.

An ordinary cookbook provides a good 'everyday' example of primary and secondary keys.

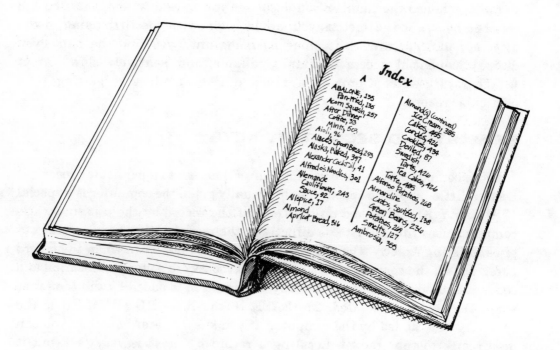

The primary key is the page number. The secondary key(s) are the names of the dishes and the ingredients. The index is the table that 'translates' the name of the food into a page number. The page number directs you to the item you want. If you knew the recipe you wanted was on page 123, that would be quicker than using the index. Using the index, however, is a lot quicker than leafing through the cookbook. You might observe more than one page number next to some of the entries. These entries are examples of non-unique keys. Secondary keys do not need to be unique.

Let's suppose that we have a database of students. Each record has the student's name, address, telephone number, room, grade, etc. We would like to be able to access student records by name or grade or room number. In order to do this we identify these three fields as secondary keys. We have three tables, one for each of the three keys. When we want a particular student's record we use the name key and request the student by name. The computer finds the name in the table, takes the record number and uses the record number to get the record from the database.

Because the tables are for a special purpose, they can be constructed to provide nearly direct access to the desired data item. In dBASE II, direct access is provided by using index files for the tables. The system will build the tables for you if the command INDEX is used. The three tables can be established like this:

```
. USE B:SCHOOL
. INDEX ON NAME TO B:NAME
. INDEX ON ROOM TO B:ROOM
. INDEX ON GRADE TO B:GRADE
```

These commands have built three tables which allow you to use the three fields NAME, ROOM and GRADE as secondary keys. The three tables have filenames B:NAME, B:ROOM, and B:GRADE. The database system adds .NDX to the end of the filename to tell the computer this is an INDEX FILE to be used for record access by the secondary key. If you need to find records according to the student's name

```
.USE B:SCHOOL INDEX B:NAME
```

You can now directly access any student record by using only the student's name with the command FIND.

```
. FIND Aardvardk, Anthony
```

Incidentally, if Anthony was the only student in the school whose last name began with Aa we could have used

```
. FIND Aa
```

which would have accomplished the same result. The computer has found the record for Anthony. To see the record just type the word DISPLAY. If you are interested in the 6th grade you would

. USE B:SCHOOL INDEX B:GRADE
. FIND 6

These two commands will get you to the first record for a 6th grade student. All of the 6th grade students will be grouped together in the order of their record numbers. Because they are grouped together you can display all 6th graders with the command

. DISPLAY WHILE GRADE='6'

When using a database with an index file (using secondary keys) the computer's execution of a command such as DISPLAY FOR GRADE='6' will be significantly slower than when using the database without the index file. Because they can be used to 'sort' records into groups, index files can be used instead of commands which physically rearrange the database — such as SORT. In addition to not affecting the physical arrangement of the database, the indexing operation is much faster than sorting.

You can also index on more than one field at a time. For example, suppose that you want to have students grouped by class (room and grade) and that you want them to be alphabetical within a class. You can use the three fields strung together as a secondary key. As an example:

. USE B:SCHOOL
. INDEX ON GRADE+ROOM+NAME TO B:CLASS

The '+' signs link the three fields together to form one key. If you were to display the entire database with the command DISPLAY ALL the students would appear in grade order by room within the grade and alphabetically within the room. The computer keeps these files on the disk so that they can be used again without having to re-index. Re-indexing can take some time, particularly if the key has several characters and the database is large. Re-indexing is only necessary if records are added or deleted or if any record has a key field changed.

Some database management systems do provide for 'automatic' re-indexing. In dBASE II this is handled by using the index files while you are adding, changing, or erasing records. In our example

. USE B:SCHOOL INDEX B:CLASS,B:NAME,B:ROOM,B:GRADE

will cause the index files B:CLASS, B:NAME, B:ROOM, AND B:GRADE to be updated each time a record is added, one of the 'key' fields is changed, or records are erased with the DELETE and PACK commands.

There are disadvantages to this. Updating multiple index files (multiple secondary keys) is slow. Very slow. This is not unique to dBASE II. Updating multiple secondary key tables in any database management system is time consuming. For this reason it is usually recommended that multiple keys (multiple index files) be avoided if at all possible. Another related disadvantage is that a change made to the database without incorporating the change into an index file can invalidate the table and any computer processing done with the use of that table.

Secondary key tables (index files), of course, require space on a disk. If you have more than one disk drive you may place an index table on a separate disk drive than the database. The tables do not need to be on the same disk as the database. However, they must be on-line. This means that the computer must have simultaneous access to the database and the index file that you are using. An index file (like a database) must be entirely contained on a single disk for most microcomputer database systems. You should consider this fact in planning your database system as well as when selecting computer hardware to support your database system.

PHYSICAL RECORDS AND LOGICAL RECORDS

In Chapter I we used the operation of an automotive parts store as an analogy to explain the concept of a database management system. In the analogy the clerk, his parts catalogs, and the storage bins to hold the auto parts are analogous to the DBMS while the actual parts are analogous to the information that is stored in the database. As you begin to read more about database systems you will find references to PHYSICAL RECORDS and LOGICAL RECORDS. Physical records are the actual data records — they correspond to the auto parts in the analogy. Logical records are the entries in the secondary key tables (index files) that tell the computer where the physical record is located on the disk. These records correspond to the entries in the clerk's catalogs that tell him where the auto parts are located.

In Chapter I we also used a library as an analogy to a database management system. In the library example, the physical records correspond to the books. The logical records correspond to the cards in the library card catalog.

In our library example, there is also another set of logical records that is used to keep track of the books. These are the book 'check out' cards. There are times when, at the library, a book that you want is out. The librarian can consult these records to tell you when the book is due to be returned. If you so desire, the book can be reserved and you will be notified when the book has been returned. It will be held a limited period of time for you.

RECORD LOCKOUT

As in the library example, more than one person may want or need to use a physical record at the same time. It is not normally desireable for more than one person to use a database record at any one time. To illustrate, suppose the database contains the seating availability on an airline flight. If two ticket agents were to use that flight information at the same time it would be possible for them to sell two separate customers the last seat on the flight. To guard against this sort of thing happening, the DBMS 'checks out' the record to the first requestor. A second requestor will be informed that the record is currently in use. The DBMS will 'reserve' the record for the second requestor's use as soon as it becomes available. All requestors of this record are said to be 'locked out' from access to that record until it has been released by the first user. The technical term for this is RECORD LOCKOUT.

It is, at present, unusual for a microcomputer database management system to provide the capability for record lockout. Most current microcomputer systems are designed to be used by only one person at a time — the personal computer. There is a growing tendency, however, for microcomputers to be shared by more than one person at a time. This allows relatively expensive and normally under-utilized peripherals, such as a printer, to be 'shared.' As database management systems become more widely used on microcomputer systems they too will contribute towards encouraging the use of multi-user microcomputers. This provides the organization with the ability to 'share' information. The ability to share information rapidly and inexpensively is of enormous value. This is the basic reason behind the development of database management systems for large mainframe computers. It is likely to become the reason for the development of affordable hardware systems to support pooled information for the smaller organization.

CHAPTER IX

THINGS YOU MIGHT
WANT TO KNOW ABOUT

PART II

There are three basic kinds of database systems.

RELATIONAL

HIERARCHICAL

and

NETWORK

A basic difference between the three is in YOUR VIEW of the way the data is organized. We think of data in tables — with rows and columns — in a relational system. The stacking hierarchy of a corporate organization chart is the picture we see in a hierarchical system. In imagining our view for a network system, think of the organization charts of two companies which have just merged. Most new database management systems are either RELATIONAL or a version of the NETWORK called CODASYL.

THE RELATIONAL DATABASE

This book focuses on the RELATIONAL database system because it relates so easily to everyday experience. Most microcomputer database management systems are variations on the RELATIONAL idea. The relational database system is exactly what it appears to be. Data is handled and stored in what, to most people, is a natural way. When using a relational system, a person inexperienced and unfamiliar with computer systems can produce useful work with relative ease.

An example of a simple relational database (taken from our liquor store inventory in Chapter II) is shown in Figure 9-1.

LIQUOR	BRAND	SIZE	QTY	COST	PRICE
SCOTCH	AULD COUNTRY	QUART	23	5.59	9.31
SCOTCH	AULD COUNTRY	2 LITER	7	9.78	16.30
SCOTCH	AULD COUNTRY	PINT	88	2.74	4.56
VODKA	REAL RUSSIAN	QUART	35	3.78	6.30
VODKA	REAL RUSSIAN	2 LITER	9	7.95	13.25
VODKA	REAL RUSSIAN	PINT	75	1.49	2.48
WHISKEY	SOUTHERN RYE	QUART	32	5.11	8.51
WHISKEY	OLD WYOMING	PINT	44	1.98	3.30
WHISKEY	OLD WYOMING	QUART	19	5.29	8.81
WHISKEY	THE NEW SOUTH	QUART	4	7.49	12.48
BOURBON	SOUTHERN ARISTOCRACY	PINT	5	0.99	1.65
BOURBON	SOUTHERN ARISTOCRACY	FIFTH	22	1.78	2.96
BOURBON	SOUTHERN ARISTOCRACY	QUART	21	3.50	5.83
BOURBON	SOUTHERN ARISTOCRACY	1/2 GAL	3	6.89	11.48
BOURBON	SOUTHERN ARISTOCRACY	2 LITER	5	6.47	10.78

Figure 9-1. Example Of A Relational Database

This relational database looks just as it would if you were to take the inventory using pencil and paper. Each record has a fixed length. Each field within the record is always the same size.

THE HIERARCHICAL DATABASE

HIERARCHICAL database systems require you to think of the data as being arranged in a hierarchy. A diagram of a hierarchical database resembles an organization chart. It also resembles an upside down tree. Hierarchical structures are often called tree structures. The liquor store database could be represented as shown in Figure 9-2.

150

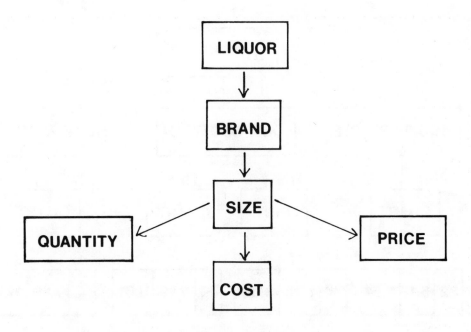

Figure 9-2. Hierarchical Representation Of Liquor Store Inventory

When represented in this way the hierarchical structure becomes apparent. Each data item is subordinant to another data item (except of course for that in the topmost box). The 'record' instead of being a simple collection of fields is a collection of subrecords or 'segments.' Each box in the example is a 'segment' or piece of the record. A segment may contain more than one field. The bottom three boxes, for example, might be grouped together to form a single segment.

The use of the word record is somewhat unfortunate since it is difficult to separate one kind of 'record' from another in our thinking. In this particular version of our liquor store database we have four 'records': one for each of the four different kinds of liquor represented in the relational database B:INVENTRY: (scotch, vodka, whiskey, and bourbon.) The hierarchical 'whiskey' record, corresponding to the 'whiskey' entries in our relational database, is shown in Figure 9-3.

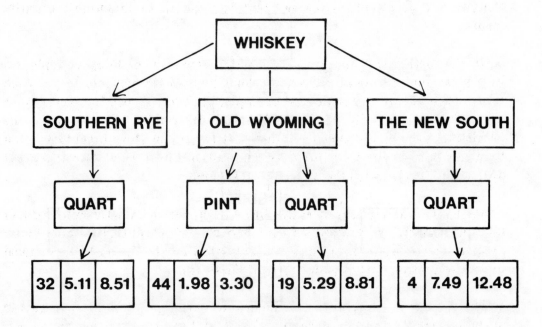

Figure 9-3. A Hierarchical 'Whiskey' Record

In these systems each segment must belong to another segment. No segment may belong to more than one segment. However, a segment may own more than one segment. Owners are often called parents. The subordinate segments are often referred to as children. In the example of Figure 9-3, Whiskey is the parent of Old Wyoming, Southern Rye, and The New South. Each of these, in turn, is the parent (or owner) of various SIZE segments. They are also the CHILDREN of 'Whiskey.'

Now let's see how this might work. Each segment has an identification code attached to it. That code is unique for each segment (primary key). It identifies the kind of segment and the sequence number (similar in concept to dBASE II's record number).

Each of the four LIQUOR segments contains several pointers. Each pointer directs the computer to a BRAND segment that 'belongs' to that LIQUOR segment. Each of these BRAND segments, in turn, contains pointers which direct the computer to each of the SIZE segments which belong to that BRAND. Each of these, in turn contain pointers which direct the computer to the segments which contain QUANTITY, COST, and PRICE. These segments may contain no pointers. Pointers allow the computer to go directly from segment to segment to assemble the entire record.

On the surface this appears to be a complicated way of doing a simple job. In a relational database system we don't have these pointers to put each record together. In our relational example, however, we use four records for the 'Whiskey' inventory. In the Hierarchical version we need only one 'Whiskey' segment plus some pointers. If our liquor store inventory has a thousand entries and there are only ten kinds of liquor we will avoid a great deal of duplication with the hierarchical system.

Saving a lot of duplication seems like a good idea. What's the rub? First of all, duplication is reduced at the expense of simplicity. While many applications fit easily into this structure, many do not. In addition, you need to decide 'up front' what your applications will be.

The fact that a segment can belong to only one parent is one rather obvious drawback to the hierarchical system. Let's suppose that we have a personnel database that is hierarchical. Two of our employees marry and have a child. The database record segment for that child cannot belong to the personnel records of both parents. Now, of course, that is silly and many artifices have been worked out to cope with this example. Nevertheless, it is illustrative of a classic shortcoming of the hierarchical system.

Telephone directory yellow pages provide a rough analogy from the paper database world to a hierarchical database. If we represent the yellow pages as shown in Figure 9-4, the hierarchical nature becomes evident.

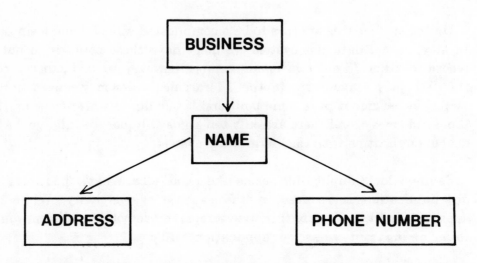

Figure 9-4. Hierarchical Representation Of The Yellow Pages

ADDRESS and PHONE NUMBER belong to the name, the NAME, in turn, belongs to the BUSINESS. Starting from the other end, BUSINESS is the owner of NAME. NAME, in turn, is the owner of both ADDRESS and PHONE NUMBER. A segment cannot belong to more than one owner. An owner, however, may own many other segments.

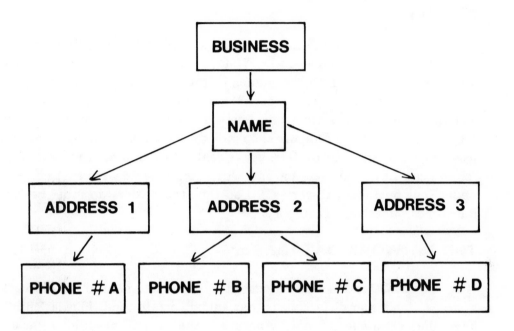

Figure 9-5

Unlike the relational database, records can be of varying sizes. Some records, for example, might have several telephone numbers while others have only one. This situation can be handled by a relational database but it requires that you either 'waste' memory or become clever. For businesses that have more than one address and/or phone number the structure might be diagrammed as shown in Figure 9-5.

To get a better idea of this, suppose we have a record of new car dealers. The BUSINESS segment contains the title 'New Car Dealers' plus pointers to direct the computer to all of the segments that contain names of new car dealers. One of these dealers is 'Vroom Vroom Motors.' The segment for 'Vroom Vroom Motors' contains the company's name as well as a set of pointers leading the computer to the addresses of the company's facilities. The database system may use the segment ID to keep order within a record (i.e. keep company names in alphabetical order). Each address segment will contain the address and the pointers for the phone numbers. A segment will always contain pointers that direct the computer to segments belonging to it. A segment MIGHT contain a pointer to lead the computer to its owner segment.

There are some possible shortcomings to the hierarchical database system — from the user's viewpoint. First of all, if we were to require an alphabetical listing of all the names in the database it would, most likely, require a substantial effort. Secondly, it is quite possible that a company would belong to more than one business category. Vroom Vroom Motors might very well have a repair shop, a body shop, a parts department, and a used car lot in addition to its new car dealership. In a hierarchical system a 'child' can have only one parent. Our sample car dealer should be listed under four business categories. To do this, the dealership must be entered four times, once in each category.

THE NETWORK DATABASE

NETWORK database management systems are similar to hierarchical systems. One major difference is that, under certain conditions, a 'child' can have more than one 'parent.' Another is that a 'parent-child' relationship such as BUSINESS-NAME can be switched. Finally, the terminology is different from both the hierarchical and the relational systems.

The term NETWORK is often used interchangeably with CODASYL. This is because the most common NETWORK database systems are based upon a proposed national standard for databases. This standard was developed by the Data Base Task Group (DBTG) of the COnference on DAta SYstems Languages. CODASYL is the organization that developed the computer language COBOL. The network database is based on the concept of sets (new math). The network database is even more complex than the hierarchical, however it does provide greater flexibility.

In the NETWORK database system, the database is made up of a collection of SETS. Each set consists of a collection of records. A record is similar to a record in the relational system except that the length need not be fixed. A record can belong to more than one set. A set is a group of like items. There are several businesses (NAMES) in each business category (BUSINESS). Therefore all of the NAMES belong to the business category set. In the phone book the new car dealers such as Vroom Vroom Motors belong to the new car dealer set. Vroom Vroom Motors is called a member of the New Car Dealer set. The owner record is New Car Dealers. Every set

Every set must have an owner record. A set can consist of only one record. A record cannot belong to two occurrences of the same set type. Therefore, the situation below is not allowed.

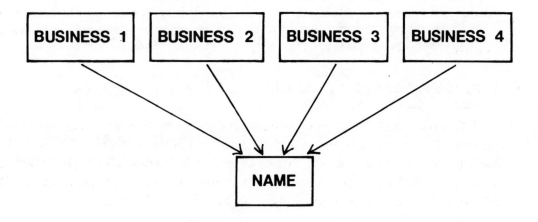

Figure 9-6

Now of course this is nonsense because we all know that a company name can show up under many business categories in the yellow pages. The problem here is that we have a situation where the number of possible relationships is enormous. It can become so enormous as to overwhelm even the largest computer. The network database is comfortable when dealing with one to many relationships. The problem is to restructure the sets so that all relationships are one to many.

A particular characteristic of the hierarchical database system was that if NAME belonged to BUSINESS, an alphabetical listing of all of the names might be difficult to do. This is because the NAMES are alphabetized for each business category and can only be accessed by business category. In the Network system NAME can belong to BUSINESS and at the same time the BUSINESS can belong to NAME.

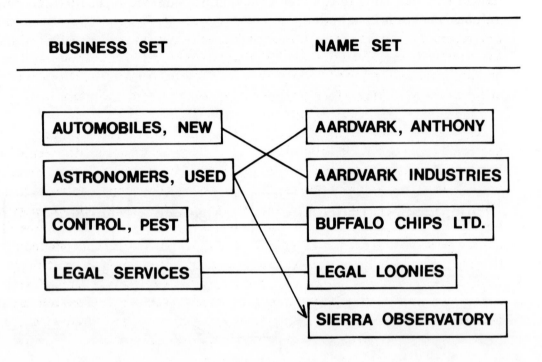

BUSINESS SET	NAME SET

Figure 9-7

As you might have expected, the network database uses an entirely different terminology from either the hierarchical or the relational database systems. The 'data item' is similar to what we have been calling a field. In the hierarchical database example there might be several phone numbers 'belonging' to an address. This is called a 'vector data aggregate.' There might also be several addresses belonging to a name. Each of the addresses has a phone number. The address-phone number is called a group. If there is more than one group it is a repeating group.

HIERARCHICAL and NETWORK database systems are substantially different in structure from the RELATIONAL system. The way that data records are structured in these systems is much more complex than the relational system. These systems are well suited to large, complex database applications. Because of this, they are used extensively on large computers. This is because they can be very efficient in the use of the computer resources — CPU time and main memory. The potential efficiency they offer can become extremely important when the database contains tens or hundreds of thousands of records. Since the cost of operating a large mainframe computer system can easily amount to several hundred dollars an hour the value of efficiency is readily apparent. The cost of professional programmers to work with these database systems is easily justified when their efforts can reduce the cost of using the database management system on this kind of computer installation. It is not apparent that this kind of efficiency is as valuable for databases to be used on microcomputers.

As was stated earlier, each of the three database systems can accommodate all of the required database functions. Each has its strengths and weaknesses. The hierarchical/network systems offer the user efficiency and speed. They are conservative in the use of the computer's resources. They are, however, complex and relatively inflexible. They were developed for use on large mainframe computer systems where billions of bytes of on-line disk storage are not uncommon. A billion bytes represents one to four thousand 8 inch floppy diskettes. Just reading that much storage at floppy disk read speed could take a half million seconds. That is DAYS. If your database needs are truly this large, a microcomputer database system may not be for you. It is not at all inconceivable that you need either a hierarchical or network database system and a large computer.

Each of the three kinds of database systems has things that it does best. Each has strengths and weaknesses. Each can perform **any** database task. The network and hierarchical approaches to database systems require that you represent the data as either a hierarchy or a network. This requires that you must 'design' your database to satisfy a particular way of using the data. What this means to you is that when you 'create' the database you must have already decided how you will use it. The relational approach requires that you represent the data in terms of tables of rows and columns. The ways in which the data is used can be determined later.

160

CHAPTER X

A LITTLE LOGIC

Computers and database management systems are built on the use of logic. Most microcomputer database systems are designed so this use of logic occurs in a very natural way. The use of logic isn't difficult — in fact it's kind of fun. However you feel about it, understanding computer logic allows you to get far more from your computer and your database management system.

There are three commonly used logical terms, referred to as logical operators.

.AND.
.OR.
.NOT.

As we mentioned earlier in this book, these are very similar to their ordinary English counterparts. The periods at each end of the word are part of the logical operator.

To illustrate the use of these terms we will use the liquor store inventory from the example in Chapter II. The database is shown in Figure 10-1.

A Little Logic

LIQUOR	BRAND	SIZE	QTY	COST	PRICE
SCOTCH	AULD COUNTRY	QUART	23	5.59	9.31
SCOTCH	AULD COUNTRY	2 LITER	7	9.78	16.30
SCOTCH	AULD COUNTRY	PINT	88	2.74	4.56
VODKA	REAL RUSSIAN	QUART	35	3.78	6.30
VODKA	REAL RUSSIAN	2 LITER	9	7.95	13.25
VODKA	REAL RUSSIAN	PINT	75	1.49	2.48
WHISKEY	SOUTHERN RYE	QUART	32	5.11	8.51
WHISKEY	OLD WYOMING	PINT	44	1.98	3.30
WHISKEY	OLD WYOMING	QUART	19	5.29	8.81
WHISKEY	THE NEW SOUTH	QUART	4	7.49	12.48
BOURBON	SOUTHERN ARISTOCRACY	PINT	5	0.99	1.65
BOURBON	SOUTHERN ARISTOCRACY	FIFTH	22	1.78	2.96
BOURBON	SOUTHERN ARISTOCRACY	QUART	21	3.50	5.83
BOURBON	SOUTHERN ARISTOCRACY	1/2 GAL	3	6.89	11.48
BOURBON	SOUTHERN ARISTOCRACY	2 LITER	5	6.47	10.78

Figure 10-1. Liquor Store Inventory

Suppose you wanted to see all the entries for WHISKEY and BOURBON. The natural tendency is to write the query command as:

DISPLAY FOR LIQUOR='BOURBON'.AND.LIQUOR='WHISKEY'

Unfortunately this won't work. This command tells the computer to display all the records where the LIQUOR field contains WHISKEY *and* BOURBON. There are none. Computer logic applies to one record at a time — not the entire database. The correct command is:

DISPLAY FOR LIQUOR='BOURBON'.OR.LIQUOR='WHISKEY'

The section of the example database this applies to is shown by the non-crosshatched area in Figure 10-2.

162

LIQUOR	BRAND	SIZE	QTY	COST	PRICE
SCOTCH	AULD COUNTRY	QUART	23	5.59	9.31
SCOTCH	AULD COUNTRY	2 LITER	7	9.78	16.30
SCOTCH	AULD COUNTRY	PINT	88	2.74	4.56
VODKA	REAL RUSSIAN	QUART	35	3.78	6.30
VODKA	REAL RUSSIAN	2 LITER	9	7.95	13.25
VODKA	REAL RUSSIAN	PINT	75	1.49	2.48
WHISKEY	SOUTHERN RYE	QUART	32	5.11	8.51
WHISKEY	OLD WYOMING	PINT	44	1.98	3.30
WHISKEY	OLD WYOMING	QUART	19	5.29	8.81
WHISKEY	THE NEW SOUTH	QUART	4	7.49	12.48
BOURBON	SOUTHERN ARISTOCRACY	PINT	5	0.99	1.65
BOURBON	SOUTHERN ARISTOCRACY	FIFTH	22	1.78	2.96
BOURBON	SOUTHERN ARISTOCRACY	QUART	21	3.50	5.83
BOURBON	SOUTHERN ARISTOCRACY	1/2 GAL	3	6.89	11.48
BOURBON	SOUTHERN ARISTOCRACY	2 LITER	5	6.47	10.78

Figure 10-2

Proper use of the .AND. operator finds the common area of two groups. For example, to determine what records contain pints of whiskey, the command is:

DISPLAY FOR LIQUOR='WHISKEY'.AND.SIZE='PINT'

The order of the fields doesn't matter. The same result is obtained by:

DISPLAY FOR SIZE='PINT'.AND.LIQUOR='WHISKEY'

If we used .OR. instead of .AND. in this last example, we would obtain an entirely different result.

DISPLAY FOR SIZE='PINT'.OR.LIQUOR='WHISKEY'

The non-crosshatched area of Figure 10-3 indicates records that would display based on this command construction.

LIQUOR	BRAND	SIZE	QTY	COST	PRICE
SCOTCH	AULD COUNTRY	QUART	23	5.59	9.31
SCOTCH	AULD COUNTRY	2 LITER	7	9.78	16.30
SCOTCH	AULD COUNTRY	PINT	88	2.74	4.56
VODKA	REAL RUSSIAN	QUART	35	3.78	6.30
VODKA	REAL RUSSIAN	2 LITER	9	7.95	13.25
VODKA	REAL RUSSIAN	PINT	75	1.49	2.48
WHISKEY	SOUTHERN RYE	QUART	32	5.11	8.51
WHISKEY	OLD WYOMING	PINT	44	1.98	3.30
WHISKEY	OLD WYOMING	QUART	19	5.29	8.81
WHISKEY	THE NEW SOUTH	QUART	4	7.49	12.48
BOURBON	SOUTHERN ARISTOCRACY	PINT	5	0.99	1.65
BOURBON	SOUTHERN ARISTOCRACY	FIFTH	22	1.78	2.96
BOURBON	SOUTHERN ARISTOCRACY	QUART	21	3.50	5.83
BOURBON	SOUTHERN ARISTOCRACY	1/2 GAL	3	6.89	11.48
BOURBON	SOUTHERN ARISTOCRACY	2 LITER	6	6.47	10.78

Figure 10-3

Suppose we want to extract those records that are pints of either whiskey or bourbon. The way to set up the command is:

DISPLAY FOR (LIQUOR='WHISKEY'.OR.LIQUOR='BOURBON').AND.SIZE='PINT'

The records that qualify under this criteria are shown in the unshaded areas of Figure 10-4.

LIQUOR	BRAND	SIZE	QTY	COST	PRICE
SCOTCH	AULD COUNTRY	QUART	23	5.59	9.31
SCOTCH	AULD COUNTRY	2 LITER	7	9.78	16.30
SCOTCH	AULD COUNTRY	PINT	88	2.74	4.56
VODKA	REAL RUSSIAN	QUART	35	3.78	6.30
VODKA	REAL RUSSIAN	2 LITER	9	7.95	13.25
VODKA	REAL RUSSIAN	PINT	75	1.49	2.48
WHISKEY	SOUTHERN RYE	QUART	32	5.11	8.51
WHISKEY	OLD WYOMING	PINT	44	1.98	3.30
WHISKEY	OLD WYOMING	QUART	19	5.29	8.81
WHISKEY	THE NEW SOUTH	QUART	4	7.49	12.48
BOURBON	SOUTHERN ARISTOCRACY	PINT	5	0.99	1.65
BOURBON	SOUTHERN ARISTOCRACY	FIFTH	22	1.78	2.96
BOURBON	SOUTHERN ARISTOCRACY	QUART	21	3.50	5.83
BOURBON	SOUTHERN ARISTOCRACY	1/2 GAL	3	6.89	11.48
BOURBON	SOUTHERN ARISTOCRACY	2 LITER	5	6.47	10.78

Figure 10-4

Suppose you inadvertently omitted the parentheses in the last example. The command would have read

DISPLAY FOR LIQUOR='WHISKEY'.OR.LIQUOR='BOURBON'.AND.SIZE='PINT'

The resulting display — which is entirely different — is shown in Figure 10-5. This happens because the .AND. operator takes precedence over the .OR. operator.

LIQUOR	BRAND	SIZE	QTY	COST	PRICE
SCOTCH	AULD COUNTRY	QUART	23	5.59	9.31
SCOTCH	AULD COUNTRY	2 LITER	7	9.78	16.30
SCOTCH	AULD COUNTRY	PINT	88	2.74	4.56
VODKA	REAL RUSSIAN	QUART	35	3.78	6.30
VODKA	REAL RUSSIAN	2 LITER	9	7.95	13.25
VODKA	REAL RUSSIAN	PINT	75	1.49	2.48
WHISKEY	SOUTHERN RYE	QUART	32	5.11	8.51
WHISKEY	OLD WYOMING	PINT	44	1.98	3.30
WHISKEY	OLD WYOMING	QUART	19	5.29	8.81
WHISKEY	THE NEW SOUTH	QUART	4	7.49	12.48
BOURBON	SOUTHERN ARISTOCRACY	PINT	5	0.99	1.65
BOURBON	SOUTHERN ARISTOCRACY	FIFTH	22	1.78	2.96
BOURBON	SOUTHERN ARISTOCRACY	QUART	21	3.50	5.83
BOURBON	SOUTHERN ARISTOCRACY	1/2 GAL	3	6.89	11.48
BOURBON	SOUTHERN ARISTOCRACY	2 LITER	5	6.47	10.78

Figure 10-5

The logical arrangement resulting in the unshaded areas of Figure 10-4 is due to the command structure

DISPLAY FOR (LIQUOR='WHISKEY'.OR.LIQUOR='BOURBON').AND.SIZE='PINT'

Now suppose you really want everything else. This can get messy if you try to write out the logic. However, you can handle this with ease by using the .NOT. operator. The command becomes

DISPLAY FOR .NOT.((LIQUOR='WHISKEY'.OR.LIQUOR='BOURBON').AND
.SIZE='PINT')

The entire logical expression is placed in parentheses to tell the computer that the .NOT. applies to everything. The result is shown in the unshaded areas of Figure 10-6.

LIQUOR	BRAND	SIZE	QTY	COST	PRICE
SCOTCH	AULD COUNTRY	QUART	23	5.59	9.31
SCOTCH	AULD COUNTRY	2 LITER	7	9.78	16.30
SCOTCH	AULD COUNTRY	PINT	88	2.74	4.56
VODKA	REAL RUSSIAN	QUART	35	3.78	6.30
VODKA	REAL RUSSIAN	2 LITER	9	7.95	13.25
VODKA	REAL RUSSIAN	PINT	75	1.49	2.48
WHISKEY	SOUTHERN RYE	QUART	32	5.11	8.51
WHISKEY	OLD WYOMING	PINT	44	1.98	3.30
WHISKEY	OLD WYOMING	QUART	19	5.29	8.81
WHISKEY	THE NEW SOUTH	QUART	4	7.49	12.48
BOURBON	SOUTHERN ARISTOCRACY	PINT	5	0.99	1.65
BOURBON	SOUTHERN ARISTOCRACY	FIFTH	22	1.78	2.96
BOURBON	SOUTHERN ARISTOCRACY	QUART	21	3.50	5.83
BOURBON	SOUTHERN ARISTOCRACY	1/2 GAL	3	6.89	11.48
BOURBON	SOUTHERN ARISTOCRACY	2 LITER	5	6.47	10.78

Figure 10-6

Now let's suppose we need to see all whiskey and bourbon records for all sizes except quarts. This is accomplished by

DISPLAY FOR (LIQUOR='WHISKEY'.OR.LIQUOR='BOURBON').AND..NOT
.SIZE='QUART'

The records affected are shown in the unshaded areas of Figure 10-7.

LIQUOR	BRAND	SIZE	QTY	COST	PRICE
SCOTCH	AULD COUNTRY	QUART	23	5.59	9.31
SCOTCH	AULD COUNTRY	2 LITER	7	9.78	16.30
SCOTCH	AULD COUNTRY	PINT	88	2.74	4.56
VODKA	REAL RUSSIAN	QUART	35	3.78	6.30
VODKA	REAL RUSSIAN	2 LITER	9	7.95	13.25
VODKA	REAL RUSSIAN	PINT	75	1.49	2.48
WHISKEY	SOUTHERN RYE	QUART	32	5.11	8.51
WHISKEY	OLD WYOMING	PINT	44	1.98	3.30
WHISKEY	OLD WYOMING	QUART	19	5.29	8.81
WHISKEY	THE NEW SOUTH	QUART	4	7.49	12.48
BOURBON	SOUTHERN ARISTOCRACY	PINT	5	0.99	1.65
BOURBON	SOUTHERN ARISTOCRACY	FIFTH	22	1.78	2.96
BOURBON	SOUTHERN ARISTOCRACY	QUART	21	3.50	5.83
BOURBON	SOUTHERN ARISTOCRACY	1/2 GAL	3	6.89	11.48
BOURBON	SOUTHERN ARISTOCRACY	2 LITER	5	6.47	10.78

Figure 10-7

You can often use characteristics of the language to help you avoid some of the more complicated logic. For example,

DISPLAY FOR LIQUOR$'BOURBON   ,WHISKEY'

will produce the same result as

DISPLAY FOR LIQUOR='BOURBON'.OR.LIQUOR='WHISKEY'

The first statement tells the computer to display each record where the content of the field LIQUOR is contained in the 'character string'. The blank spaces are there because the computer will compare the entire field LIQUOR with the character string. The field has ten characters. If you had omitted the blank spaces the computer would not find a match with any field content. Blank spaces have as much meaning to the computer as any other character.

If you want to see everything except BOURBON or WHISKEY, the proper command is

```
DISPLAY FOR .NOT.LIQUOR$'BOURBON          ,WHISKEY'
```

The dollar sign is a shorthand way of saying 'contained in.' It is sometimes called a string operator. The extra spaces are there because the field LIQUOR has 10 spaces (width = 10). If the extra spaces were not used the computer would be unable to find a match for the field in this character string. The comma is not necessary in this case, however it is usually good practice to separate possible "matches" with some character that is not a possible match.

The use of the logical operators — .AND, .OR, and .NOT. — allows you to specify to the computer exactly what conditions apply to the commands. They improve your efficiency by having the computer screen the database records to locate the specific ones you are interested in. Later in the book, we will discuss procedures which provide you with even more help from the computer. The logical operators will become even more important as you begin to describe to the computer exactly what you want it to automatically do.

A Little Logic

SECTION FOUR

Section Four is about power, speed and ease. The computer's capability can be dramatically enhanced by teaching it some new tricks. It is not hard to teach the computer tricks — and it is really great how closely you can customize these tricks to support your specific information storing and reporting needs.

We use again familiar database examples to define menu options, utilize 'do while' clauses and automate routine activities that customize our system, giving us a greater 'reach' and saving us time and energy. The customization gives us a very important thing: the ability to produce specific reports.

CHAPTER XI

THE FINE ART OF PROCEDURES

Most database management systems have a Query Language Processor and a Report Writer. These two DBMS pieces can probably satisfy most, if not all, or your needs. Any further need is easily accommodated using simple procedures. In previous chapters, we discussed several examples of procedure generated special processes. There are lots of things you can do using procedures to construct exactly what you want the computer to do for you in a specific circumstance. This process not only makes custom, deluxe, 'designed-for-you' computer output, but also is a very practical way to save you work.

To illustrate how a procedure can save you effort we will work through a simple example of a Check Register database. This sample database, B:CHECKREG, has a plan which is shown as Figure 11-1.

FIELD	FIELD DESCRIPTION	FIELDNAME	TYPE	WIDTH	DECIMALS
1	Check Number	CHECKNO	N	4	
2	Paid To	PAIDTO	C	20	
3	Amount of Check or Dep	AMOUNT	N	7	2
4	Deposit or Check	DEPOSIT	L	1	
5	Deductible (Y/N)	DEDUCT	L	1	
6	Cancelled (Y/N)	CANCEL	L	1	
7	Date (mm/dd/yy)	DATE	C	8	

Figure 11-1. Check Register Database Plan

In this particular example we have chosen to have a logic field indicate whether the amount is for a check or a deposit. A 'Y' indicates that the amount is a deposit.

To calculate the account balance, proceed with the query language dialog in Screen 11-1.

```
. SUM AMOUNT TO MDEPOSIT FOR DEPOSIT
10677.80
. SUM AMOUNT TO CHECKS FOR.NOT.DEPOSIT
9450.51
. STORE MDEPOSIT—CHECKS TO BALANCE
1227.29



                        Screen 11-1
```

Note the memory variable which stores the sum of the deposits is called MDEPOSIT. The temptation to name the variable DEPOSIT is unfortunate: a datafield and a memory variable may not have the same name. It will confuse the computer.

Note: in this example we add all of the checks and all of the deposits each time we calculate the balance. In a conventional checkbook, we usually keep a running balance. With the computer it is often easier to calculate the balance each time than to keep a running balance.

As you can see, there are three instructions required to determine the bank balance. We will likely want to know the bank balance often. To save ourselves the work and nuisance of typing 3 instructions each time we want to know the balance, we will create a means for the computer to 'remember' the instructions. A 'procedure' is our means for getting the computer to do this 'remembering.'

The computer 'remembers' a procedure, such as our example, by placing the instructions in a special kind of file. The file is placed on a disk and available whenever you want to use it. In dBASE II this special file is called a COMMAND FILE. A command file provides the capability to 'save' a group of commands so that we can use them — as a group — without retyping them each time.

To get the computer to 'remember' a procedure you must first tell it that you are going to write one. In dBASE II this is accomplished by the command MODIFY COMMAND.

.MODIFY COMMAND

The computer will respond with a request for a filename. The same filename rules apply as have applied for database files and report files. A filename must have eight or fewer letters and must begin with a letter. You should also identify which disk drive the procedure is to be stored on by using a disk drive identifier. In this example we will call the command file BALANCE and place it on the B drive.

ENTER FILE NAME: B:BALANCE

The video screen will clear. For a brief moment the screen will display

NEW FILE

The words 'NEW FILE' will disappear and the screen will be completely blank with the exception of the cursor in the upper left hand corner of the screen. There will be no dot prompt. There is nothing wrong — this is just the way the designer implemented the command.

Type in the instructions one after another just as though you are typing on a blank sheet of paper. The typed instructions appear as shown in Screen 11-2.

Note that an extra line has been added to the end of the procedure. This line contains the single word CANCEL. This is to 'return' control of the computer to the keyboard after the computer has completed the procedure.

```
SUM AMOUNT TO MDEPOSIT FOR DEPOSIT
SUM AMOUNT TO CHECKS FOR .NOT.DEPOSIT
STORE MDEPOSIT-CHECKS TO BALANCE
CANCEL
♦
```

Screen 11-2

The computer will not execute the instructions while you are writing a procedure. Since most of us are not perfect typists the system provides a limited editing capability through use of the control key. Editing capabilities and the associated control keys are shown in Figure 11-2.

CONTROL	EDITING ACTION
S	Moves cursor 1 character left
D	Moves cursor 1 character right
E	Moves cursor 1 line up
X	Moves cursor 1 line down
N	Makes a blank line
T	Deletes a line
Y	Erases contents of a line
G	Deletes a character
V	Inserts characters
W	Saves the procedure on disk and returns the keyboard to normal operation
Q	Discards the procedure and returns keyboard to normal operation

Figure 11-2. Editing Capabilities For MODIFY COMMAND

When commands have been typed in as shown in Screen 11-2, simply press CONTROL and W at the same time. This causes the COMMAND FILE named 'BALANCE' to be written on the B disk: you can use it as often as you desire.

You can use the procedure B:BALANCE any time the check register database is in use. To have the computer do the procedure B:BALANCE, type 'DO' followed by B:BALANCE, as shown in Screen 11-3. Note that the result of each instruction is displayed — the instructions themselves are not. This is certainly easier than typing the instructions each time we want the balance.

```
. DO B:BALANCE
10677.80
9450.51
1227.29
DO CANCELLED
◆
```

Screen 11-3

This is terrific. We only have to type in a couple of words (DO: B:BALANCE) and the answer appears. We may have one small problem: how to remember which number is which. The solution is really easy. We simply have the computer display the instructions as well as the answers as in Screen 11-1. The instructions are displayed by using a command 'SET ECHO ON.' In general, commands are not displayed. however, as in this case, there are situations where it is desirable to see the commands.

So, we want to add to our 'procedure' this request to see the instruction sequence. We insert 'SET ECHO ON' into our existing procedure B:BALANCE by using the command 'MODIFY COMMAND.'

```
.MODIFY COMMAND
  ENTER FILE NAME:B:BALANCE
```

The screen will be erased and the existing file B:BALANCE will be displayed. The cursor will be positioned at the upper left corner of the screen directly on the 'S' of the first SUM. The command SET ECHO ON is placed on the first line by pressing CONTROL N — which provides a blank line — and then typing SET ECHO ON. Use CONTROL X to move the cursor to the first C of the word CANCEL. Press CONTROL N, providing you with a blank line, then type in SET ECHO OFF (the normal condition). The screen should appear as shown in Screen 11-4.

```
SET ECHO ON
SUM AMOUNT TO MDEPOSIT FOR DEPOSIT
SUM AMOUNT TO CHECKS FOR .NOT.DEPOSIT
STORE MDEPOSIT-CHECKS TO BALANCE
SET ECHO OFF
CANCEL
◆
```

Screen 11-4

Press CONTROL W to save the new command file BALANCE on disk drive B. Now, whenever you have the computer execute the procedure B:BALANCE, the results will appear as shown in Screen 11-5.

```
. SUM AMOUNT TO MDEPOSIT FOR DEPOSIT
10677.80
. SUM AMOUNT TO CHECKS FOR .NOT.DEPOSIT
9450.51
. STORE MDEPOSIT—CHECKS TO BALANCE
1227.29
```

Screen 11-5

Writing a procedure uses the same 'mechanics' as writing a letter. The difference, of course, is that a procedure is written on the computer using a language the computer understands. Most microcomputer database management systems allow you to write procedures in two ways: via an internal feature of the DBMS or using a word processing system separate from the DBMS.

A word processing system is a special software system designed specifically for working with text.

When you use a word processing system to write a procedure, you must type in a FILE IDENTIFIER in addition to the filename and disk drive identifier. A FILE IDENTIFIER consists of a period followed by three letters. When working 'inside' dBASE II, this file identifier is assigned automatically — dBASE 'knows' what kind of a file you're making by the commands you give it and attaches the .CMD identifier for you. When working from a word processing system, the file identifier must be typed in as part of the name. The word processing system does not know about kinds of files.

In dBASE II the file identifier for procedures (command files) is '.CMD'. This FILE IDENTIFIER permits the database system to know that the file is a procedure. Our sample procedure (command file) would be named

B:BALANCE.CMD

when prepared on a word processing system.

Even if the procedure can be written from within the database system, it is often advantageous to write it with a word processing system. Word processing systems generally offer significantly greater editing capabilities than are available with the DBMS. After all, that's what word processing systems are for. These editing features are of great value when writing lengthy procedures.

Word processing systems usually provide a special mode for use when preparing material to be read by the computer. All procedures, command files and computer programs prepared on a word processing system must be written using this mode. The normal word processing mode for preparing letters and documents adds symbols to the text that you cannot see. These are for its internal use in editing and subsequently printing the letters and documents. These extra symbols can cause problems if they are inadvertently included in a procedure. If you are not sure which mode to use, consult the user's manual for the word processing system you are using.

SAVE YOURSELF SOME TIME AND MINOR IRRITATION

When the computer executes an instruction such as SUM it must 'read' the entire database from the disk. The time it takes to read the database depends primarily on the size of the database and the kind of disk drive. A typical floppy disk drive might read the database at 1600 characters per second. A very small database of 16000 characters will take 10 seconds each time that it is read. One of 160,000 characters will take 100 seconds.

If you are entering commands manually you will find that the short delay for the computer to read the database becomes very annoying if the delay is more than about 5 seconds. Because of this 'read' time, it is often beneficial to group commands. Whenever entering a number of manual commands, it is often convenient to place the commands into a procedure. This will free you from the annoying short waits of a few to several seconds for each instruction.

The idea behind establishing a procedure is to have the computer do all (or at least most) of the work. You give it a list of single instructions — it does them for you all at once. You are the boss. It is the uncomplaining, loyal slave. If you normally sit at a computer keyboard and interrogate the computer about the contents of your database, you can save yourself a lot of time if you write a procedure that has the computer do what you want it to.

For instance, suppose you want to acquire a lot of information about scotch and gin from our liquor store inventory database. You can sit at the keyboard and enter a series of commands — OR, you can write a procedure that is a list of those commands and the computer will do it for you.

```
COUNT FOR LIQUOR='SCOTCH'
COUNT FOR LIQUOR='GIN'
COUNT FOR LIQUOR='SCOTCH'.AND.SIZE='FIFTH'
etc.
```

If you enter these commands from the keyboard it takes the computer a few seconds to respond to each of them. If the database is large, it may take many seconds for each response. If you enter the commands as a procedure you can relax and have a cup of coffee while the computer gets you the answers you want. The time it takes the computer might not be any less but YOU aren't sitting around twiddling your thumbs while the computer searches for the answers.

We are all familiar with some set of instructions that must be followed explicitly. This kind of set of instructions is what the computer uses. If the computer is to be able to follow the procedure, we must write the instructions in a way the computer can understand. Remember, the computer may be very, very fast, but it isn't very bright. A computer procedure must be written very clearly. You may not assume that the computer 'knows' anything.

To really get a feeling for this consider the following example. If we ask a very small child to count to three he can probably manage to do it. To get the computer to count to three is something else. The computer can only count to three if we 'teach' it — give it a procedure — to count to three. Even after it's done it once, it won't be able to do it again unless the procedure is used.

To illustrate this, an ordinary English version of a computer procedure to count to three is shown below. This procedure is very similar to the procedure a person might follow if using a hand calculator with a memory.

Step 1. Store a 'zero' in memory

Step 2. Add 1 to the contents of the memory and store the result in memory

Step 3. Display the contents of the memory

Step 4. Add 1 to the contents of the memory and store the result in memory

Step 5. Display the contents of the memory

Step 6. Add 1 to the contents of the memory and store the result in memory

Step 7. Display the contents of the memory

The Fine Art of Procedures

When we want the computer to perform this procedure, it must be written differently. The 'translation' of our English to a computer language will be different for each computer language, just as it would differ if we were translating into some other human language such as French or German. In dBASE II's Application Development Language (ADL) it will look like this.

Step 1.   STORE 0 TO X
Steps 2 and 3. STORE X + 1 TO X
Steps 4 and 5. STORE X + 1 TO X
Steps 6 and 7. STORE X + 1 TO X

The procedure itself contains only the terms starting with the word STORE. The step numbers are shown so that you can easily see the correspondence between the two versions of the procedure.

You should notice two things about this sample procedure.

- First, we are doing the same thing over and over.

- Second, this approach isn't very practical for doing the same thing a large number of times — like counting to a thousand.

The English version can be rewritten like:

Step 1. Store a 'zero' in memory

Step 2. Add 1 to the contents of the memory and store the result in memory

Step 3. Display the contents of the memory

Step 4. Repeat step 2

Step 5. Repeat step 3

Step 6. Repeat step 2

Step 7. Repeat step 3

In A. A. Milne's book Winnie The Poo Winnie and Piglet discover footprints in the snow in front of Piglet's house. Dreaming of great adventure, the two set out to follow the tracks and see where they might lead

182

and what sort of creature might have made them. They follow these footprints on and on until, at last, they find themselves back at Piglet's house. There they find three sets of footprints leading away from Piglet's house. One set is much smaller than the other two. After some debate they speculate that they are tracking a woozle and a wizzle. Off they go again following the footprints. After a time they find two more sets of footprints have joined the first three. Piglet becomes quite concerned over his safety and discovers he has work to do at home. He leaves. Winnie the Poo finally determines the footprints are their own . . . they have been going in circles.

In the case of Winnie the Poo and Piglet, going in circles might have been high adventure but it really got them nowhere. In our case, however, it turns out that going in circles will get us farther faster. Circles facilitate writing simple procedures.

DO WHILE . . . ENDDO

Simplification # 1

    Step 1. Store a 'zero' in memory

    Step 2. Add 1 to the content of the memory and store the result in memory

    Step 3. Display the content of the memory

    Step 4. If memory is less than 3 go to step 2

Simplification # 2

    Step 1. Store a 'zero' in memory

    Step 2. Do steps 3 and 4 as long as the content of the memory is less than 3

    Step 3. Add 1 to the content of the memory and store the result in memory

    Step 4. Display the content of the memory

The first example is typical of the way you might write a procedure in one of the 'traditional' computer languages such as FORTRAN, COBOL, or

**The Fine Art of
Procedures**

BASIC. The latter is representative of the 'modern' languages such as
PASCAL, PL/1, and ADL. Writing our simple counting example
(Simplification #2) in ADL we get:

```
STORE 0 TO X
DO WHILE X< 3
STORE X+1 TO X
ENDDO
```

The sideways arrow '<' is arithmetic shorthand meaning 'less than.' The
statement beginning with DO is read as 'do while X is less than 3.' The
arrow turned around ('>') means 'greater than.' The statement could be
written: 'DO WHILE 3>X' which reads 'do while 3 is greater than X.' The
two statements DO WHILE X< 3 and DO WHILE 3>X mean exactly the
same thing.

This new example has just as many instructions as the original did. There
is one important difference however — we can cause the computer to count
to a hundred or a thousand or a million just by changing the '3' to the
desired counting goal. The command DO WHILE X< 3 tells the computer
that you want it to keep repeating the following instructions as long as the
value of X is less than three. ENDDO signifies the end of the group of
instructions begun by DO WHILE. Each DO WHILE must have an ENDDO.
DO WHILE — ENDDO is one way of telling the computer to perform the
same set of instructions over and over as long as some condition [such as
X< 3:] is valid. The group of statements beginning with DO WHILE and
ending with ENDDO is called a 'LOOP.'

INITIALIZING THE LOOP

Immediately in front of the loop we used an instruction that stored the
value 0 to the memory variable X. You know if you count to three, you begin
at one. The computer doesn't know where to begin. It must be told where to
begin — as well as how to count. This single instruction — store 0 to X —
does two things:

- It stores the value of 0 to X
- It also 'creates' the memory variable X

You are not allowed to use a memory variable in a procedure until the
variable has been 'created.' Also, you are not allowed to 'create' the
memory variable without giving it an initial value. In this case the variable

was created and assigned an initial value with the instruction 'STORE 0 to X'. The statement 'initializes' the LOOP by providing the starting place and creating the variable X.

ACCUMULATOR: A BASIC CONCEPT

This simple little counting procedure is an ACCUMULATOR. The accumulator forms the basis of the ordinary adding machine and the hand held electronic calculator. It is a basic concept quite often used in procedures used with database systems business applications.

Procedures to accomplish more complex tasks are usually made up of a group of simple procedures. As an example, suppose you want to count by 1's to 10 and then by 10's to one hundred. One way to do this is to use two of our simple counting loops in succession.

```
STORE 0 TO X

DO WHILE X < 10
STORE X+1 TO X
ENDDO

DO WHILE X < 100
STORE X+10 TO X
ENDDO
```

AN ALTERNATIVE PROCEDURE: 'IF'

Another way to achieve exactly the same result is to have the computer take different actions for different values of X. This is, of course, what occurs above, however this procedure takes advantage of the fact that we know everything about X and what we want to happen. The computer is capable of making decisions — albeit limited ones. We can take advantage of this capability and write an equivalent procedure.

The Fine Art of Procedures

```
STORE 0 TO X

DO WHILE X< 100

  IF X< 10
     STORE X+1 TO X
  ENDIF

  IF X> = 10
     STORE X+10 TO X
  ENDIF

ENDDO
```

'IF' is the word we use when we want the computer to make a decision about whether or not to do something. It's used in exactly the same way we ordinarily use the word IF. IF it's raining take an umbrella; IF the gas tank is getting low stop and get gasoline. We use IF when the action to be taken (or conclusion to be drawn) depends on some condition.

In the example, the action is to add one number to another. The condition is the value of one plus the accumulator X. When the computer makes each decision it doesn't know about the other IF. Each IF must have an ENDIF just as each DO WHILE must have an ENDDO. The information after IF (X< 10) is the condition for the computer to make a decision about. The decision that it makes is whether or not X is less than 10. If it is, the IF applies and the computer will execute the instruction STORE X + 1 to X. If it isn't the computer won't store X + 1 to X.

DO WHILE and IF are the basic tools that can be used for any procedure you might require. These examples employ the specific terminology of the Application Development Language from dBASE II. The concepts, however, are universal and are used in all computer languages. The terminology is similar to that used by modern languages such as PL/1 and PASCAL.

To give you a better idea of how you can use DO WHILE and IF we will write a procedure that accomplishes the same things as B:BALANCE using these two features. We will also take this opportunity to demonstrate how you can exert more control over the displays produced by the computer. The new B:BALANCE is shown as Screen 11-6. The original results of the procedure (Screen 11-1) is reproduced here for your convenience.

```
. SUM AMOUNT TO MDEPOSIT FOR DEPOSIT
10677.80
. SUM AMOUNT TO CHECKS FOR .NOT.DEPOSIT
9450.51
. STORE MDEPOSIT — CHECKS TO BALANCE
1227.29
```

Screen 11-1

```
USE B:CHECKREG
SET TALK OFF
STORE 0 TO MDEPOSIT,CHECKS
DO WHILE .NOT.EOF
  IF DEPOSIT
       STORE AMOUNT+MDEPOSIT TO MDEPOSIT
  ENDIF
  IF .NOT.DEPOSIT
       STORE AMOUNT+CHECKS TO CHECKS
  ENDIF
SKIP
ENDDO
? 'TOTAL DEPOSITS',MDEPOSIT
? 'TOTAL CHECKS   ',CHECKS
? 'BALANCE        ',MDEPOSIT-CHECKS
SET TALK ON
CANCEL
```

Screen 11-6

In our example, we use instructions which may be unfamiliar to you

```
SET TALK OFF/ON
SKIP
DO WHILE .NOT. EOF
?
```

SET TALK OFF/ON

You may have noticed that many commands — like STORE, SUM, etc. — display a response each time they are used. This is one of the ways the computer 'talks' to you. This is desirable when you are working with the computer from your keyboard. It is often not so desirable when using procedures. It clutters up the screen (and/or the printer). In dBASE II the visual response to a command can be turned on and off. SET TALK ON and SET TALK OFF are the commands that do this.

SKIP

The database management system actually works with only one record at a time. When the USE statement is made, the DBMS is positioned to the very top of the database — Record 1. Each use of the verb SKIP will advance the DBMS one record. When the last record is reached the next use of SKIP will alert the DBMS that the end of the file has been reached.

DO WHILE .NOT.EOF

As we have seen in previous examples, the DO WHILE command applies as long as some condition is true. EOF is read as 'end of file.' The command literally means 'computer — do the following until you come to the end of the database.' This is probably the most commonly used version of DO WHILE. This will automatically stop the DO LOOP when the end of the database is reached.

?

The question mark is a versatile command providing the ability to display specific information. The apostrophes at each end of the text — such as 'TOTAL DEPOSITS' — are called delimiters. Their presence indicates that the enclosed characters are text to be displayed. The memory variable name indicates the contents of that memory variable are to be displayed. The comma is used to separate items to be displayed. Each question mark will produce one line of display.

Our new sample procedure B:BALANCE is just a little more complicated than our original version. On the other hand, a few moments work have produced a result much more tailored to our needs. When we have the computer execute this command file the display shown in Screen 11-7 is produced.

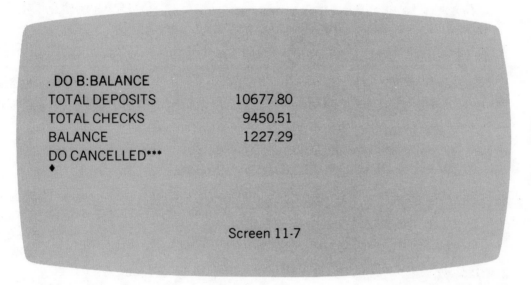

```
. DO B:BALANCE
TOTAL DEPOSITS          10677.80
TOTAL CHECKS            9450.51
BALANCE                 1227.29
DO CANCELLED***
◆
```

Screen 11-7

Procedures enable a computer to do more work for you. They are an easy way to get more work out of your computer. In this chapter we introduced some basic concepts: the accumulator, the DO loop, the decision (IF) as well as some of the dBASE II commands frequently used in procedures. Procedures like the ones in this chapter are fun to write and ultimately save you both time and effort. In addition, they reduce the chance of error. Once a procedure is correctly written it enables the computer to perform the function over and over without mistake.

**The Fine Art of
Procedures**

190

CHAPTER XII

MAKING A PROCEDURE
WORK FOR YOU

Procedures are intended to save you time, effort and money as well as provide a more satisfactory result. They can be used for virtually any purpose you can think of. 'Automating' routine activities is one of the more useful things you can make the computer do for you. After all, the computer is supposed to make life easier for you.

In this chapter, we will explore a fairly comprehensive example of what a computer plus a database management system can do. We will again stay in the realm of universal familiarity and 'computerize' an ordinary checkbook. The resulting check register process has advantages beyond mere familiarity: it can be used to demonstrate numerous ideas.

The plan for our example database B:CHECKREG is shown in Figure 12-1.

FIELD	FIELD DESCRIPTION	FIELDNAME	TYPE	WIDTH	DECIMALS
1	Check Number	CHECKNO	N	4	
2	Paid To	PAIDTO	C	20	
3	Amount of Check or Dep	AMOUNT	N	7	2
4	Deposit or Check	DEPOSIT	L	1	
5	Deductible (Y/N)	DEDUCT	L	1	
6	Cancelled (Y/N)	CANCEL	L	1	
7	Date (mm/dd/yy)	DATE	C	8	

Figure 12-1. Check Register Database Plan

The fields in this plan correspond to an ordinary check register with one major exception: there is no field provided for a running account balance. In a conventional checkbook it is vital to keep a running balance. It obviously isn't practical to balance the entire checkbook each time we use it. With the computer, however, this isn't true, as it is perfectly reasonable to do all of the bookkeeping each time we use the checkbook. This was demonstrated in Chapter XI.

There are a number of routine tasks involved in keeping any checkbook up to date. Among these are:

1. Enter a Check
2. Enter a Deposit
3. Change an entry to correct a mistake
4. See if you wrote a particular check
5. List deductible checks at tax time
6. Determine Current Balance
7. Balance (Compare to Bank Statement)

Some of these activities are performed 'as needed.' Others are done regularly, i.e., daily, monthly, yearly. All can be accomplished from your computer keyboard using the database and query language. In the long run it is more efficient — and you will feel more confident — if your checkbook maintenance is done using procedures. The procedure establishes an appropriate process — you won't have to worry about it again.

In Chapter XI we discussed the basic idea of a procedure as well as tools appropriate to implementing one. In the remainder of this chapter, we will use those ideas and tools to write a set of procedures to manage our checkbook. This set of procedures is intended to illustrate concepts. They are not a comprehensive checkbook management package.

To accomplish our objective and accommodate our routine checkbook tasks, we need a total of seven procedures. We have one of these already (number 6 — Determine Current Balance). Each of the seven is about the same size as our example B:BALANCE. And, because they are all part of the same process — managing a checkbook — it is reasonable to make them items on a menu.

Making a menu is even simpler than our example procedure B:BALANCE. To give a very quick and straightforward treatment to this process we will take our list of menu items and make the menu directly from it. The menu procedure B:BANKMENU is shown in Figure 12-2.

```
USE B:CHECKREG
INDEX ON CHECKNO TO B:CHECKNO
USE B:CHECKREG INDEX B:CHECKNO
SET TALK OFF
DO WHILE T
ERASE
?
?
? '                      CHECK REGISTER MENU'
?
? '          1.   Enter a Check'
? '          2.   Enter a Deposit'
? '          3.   Changing an entry to correct a mistake'
? '          4.   Seeing if you wrote a particular check'
? '          5.   Listing deductible checks at tax time'
? '          6.   Determine Current Balance'
? '          7.   Balancing (Compare to Bank Statement)'
? '          8.   EXIT'
?
? '        PRESS THE NUMBER CORRESPONDING TO YOUR SELECTION'
WAIT TO SELECTION
ERASE
IF SELECTION='1'
     DO B:CHECKENT
ENDIF
IF SELECTION='2'
     DO B:DEPOSITS
ENDIF
IF SELECTION='3'
     DO B:CHANGES
ENDIF
IF SELECTION='4'
     DO B:LOOK
ENDIF
IF SELECTION='5'
     DO B:DEDUCT
```

```
ENDIF
IF SELECTION='6'
    DO B:BALANCE
ENDIF
IF SELECTION='7'
    DO B:CHKBANK
ENDIF
IF SELECTION='8'
    SET TALK ON
    CANCEL
ENDIF
ENDDO
```

Figure 12-2. Check Register Menu

Once again we have introduced a few new instructions. These are:

```
DO WHILE T
ERASE
WAIT TO SELECTION
?
```

DO WHILE T

This literally means 'do forever'. The DO WHILE statement usually means do while the following condition is true. In this case 'T' (for 'true') is always true. Since we really don't want to go through this loop forever we have included menu item 8, providing an escape back to the database management system.

ERASE

This instruction erases any existing text from the screen.

WAIT TO SELECTION

The WAIT command causes a procedure to pause. The procedure will restart by pressing any character. WAIT TO SELECTION means to store the character that was pressed in the memory variable 'SELECTION' and restart the procedure. The contents of SELECTION are used to tell the computer what to do.

?

The question mark can be used in a variety of ways. When used alone it will cause a blank line to appear on the video screen or on a printer. It is also used to display the contents of memory variables and data fields.

Text that is enclosed by apostrophes or quotes will appear as text on a line. Blank spaces can be used to adjust the position of the text on the video screen or a printer.

The menu procedure works like this. Entering the command DO B:BANKMENU will cause the menu to appear on the screen as shown in Screen 12-1.

```
             CHECK REGISTER MENU

        1. Enter a Check
        2. Enter a Deposit
        3. Changing an entry to correct a mistake
        4. Seeing if you wrote a particular check
        5. Listing deductible checks at tax time
        6. Determine Current Balance
        7. Balancing (Compare to Bank Statement)
        8. EXIT


      PRESS THE NUMBER CORRESPONDING TO YOUR SELECTION

WAITING ◆



                 Screen 12-1
```

Press the number key that corresponds to your selection. This is another case where you do not need to use the RETURN key. The number you press is stored in the memory variable SELECTION as a character. The IF instruction that matches your selection causes the computer to execute a procedure. For example, if you choose item 6, the computer will execute the command file B:BALANCE.

The first set of instructions in the menu procedure (Figure 12-2) will index the database according to check number. You would not actually re-index each time you used the menu. The indexing operation is shown only to point out that the procedure is based on using an indexed database.

MENU OPTION #1

Pressing the '1' key selects menu option 1, allowing entry of a new check into your computerized checkbook. This could, of course, also be accomplished by the command APPEND, but in this example we want to illustrate a means of accomplishing the results of append while providing fully descriptive prompts for each data item.

One procedure that allows entry of a new check is shown in Figure 12-3. Again, we introduce a few new commands:

    ACCEPT
    INPUT
    RETURN
    APPEND BLANK

ACCEPT AND INPUT

ACCEPT and INPUT offer a means for the computer to 'ask' you to enter data from the keyboard during a procedure. INPUT is used to enter numeric data. ACCEPT is used to enter character data. Otherwise they are the same. The command form is demonstrated by examples in Figure 12-3. The command displays the desired text, creates a memory variable such as MCHECKNO, and waits for you to enter data into the variable.

RETURN

RETURN is similar to CANCEL in that it terminates the procedure — in this case, the check entering procedure. This returns control of the computer to the menu program B:BANKMENU, displaying the checkbook menu. CANCEL would terminate the entire operation, returning computer control to the keyboard.

APPEND BLANK

APPEND BLANK, often used with procedures, is a variation of the append command. APPEND is the only way to add a record to the database. APPEND BLANK simply adds a blank record, but does not display the record for data entry. In this example a blank record is created, data is entered into memory variables with ACCEPT and INPUT commands, and then the data is transferred from the memory variables into the blank record using the REPLACE command. It was not necessary to use SET TALK OFF since that had been previously accomplished by the menu procedure B:BANKMENU. (Figure 12-2)

In this particular example the prompts are displayed and the data entered one instruction at a time. From this standpoint the procedure is not as effective as APPEND since the cursor cannot be moved back to correct a previous data item.

```
APPEND BLANK
INPUT 'ENTER CHECK NUMBER' TO MCHECKNO
ACCEPT 'PAID TO THE ORDER OF' TO MPAIDTO
INPUT 'ENTER AMOUNT OF CHECK' TO MAMOUNT
ACCEPT 'ENTER DATE (mm/dd/yy)' TO MDATE
ACCEPT 'IS THIS CHECK DEDUCTIBLE (Y/N)' TO MDEDUCT
REPLACE CHECKNO WITH MCHECKNO, PAIDTO WITH MPAIDTO, AMOUNT
   WITH MAMOUNT, DATE WITH MDATE, DEDUCT WITH MEDEDUCT, DEPOSIT
   WITH N RETURN
```

Figure 12-3. A Preliminary Procedure for Check Entry

A computer display similar to APPEND — with more descriptive prompts replacing the fieldnames — would be far more desirable. In addition, for more relaxed data entry, the cursor should be movable backwards one or more fields to correct errors. This is accomplished, within dBASE II, using special commands provided for exactly this purpose.

The general form of the dBASE II command is:

```
@ LINE,COLUMN SAY 'WHATEVER YOU WANT' GET FIELDNAME
READ
```

The first of these, the '@' command allows data positioning control on the screen. Most computer terminals have a video screen with 24 lines of 80 characters each. The lines are numbered from top to bottom, 0 to 23. The columns (character positions) are numbered from left to right, 0 to 79. To display — THIS IS AN EXAMPLE — on line 5 beginning with column 10, the command reads

```
@ 5,10 SAY 'THIS IS AN EXAMPLE'
```

The text, 'THIS IS AN EXAMPLE' will be displayed at half-intensity just as the fieldnames are in APPEND.

Similarly, the contents of a field can be displayed by

```
@ 5,10 GET PAIDTO
```

This example displays the current contents of the field PAIDTO at full intensity — as when using the EDIT command.

The two examples can be combined as

```
@ 5,10 SAY 'THIS IS AN EXAMPLE' GET PAIDTO
```

The command READ allows you to change the field contents identified with GET. An example procedure to enter checks using these commands is shown in Figure 12-4. The display produced by this command is shown as Screen 12-2.

```
APPEND BLANK
@ 5,10 SAY 'ENTER CHECK NUMBER' GET CHECKNO
@ 7,10 SAY 'PAID TO THE ORDER OF' GET PAID TO
@ 9,10 SAY 'ENTER AMOUNT OF CHECK' GET AMOUNT
@ 11,10 SAY 'ENTER DATE (mm/dd/yy)' GET DATE
@ 13,10 SAY 'IS THIS CHECK DEDUCTIBLE (Y/N)' GET DEDUCT
READ
REPLACE DEPOSIT WITH N
RETURN
```

Figure 12-4

This procedure will cause the computer to behave in a manner very similar to APPEND except that descriptive prompts replace the fieldnames. All the CONTROL keys for moving the cursor behave just as in APPEND. Note that all fields are not displayed — only those of interest to this procedure are chosen to be displayed.

The display produced by this procedure is shown as Screen 12-2. The cursor is initially in the first character position of the CHECKNO field — ready to enter data.

```
ENTER CHECK NUMBER : ♦    :

PAID TO THE ORDER OF :                    :

ENTER AMOUNT OF CHECK :          :

ENTER DATE (mm/dd/yy) :            :

IS THIS CHECK DEDUCTIBLE (Y/N) :  :
```

Screen 12-2

Since check numbers are usually sequential you can save a small amount of bother by having the computer enter the check number for you. The revised procedure to accomplish this is shown in Figure 12-5. The changes are shown in boldfaced type.

```
GO BOTTOM
STORE CHECKNO+1 TO CNO
APPEND BLANK
REPLACE CHECKNO WITH CNO, DEPOSIT WITH N
@ 5,10 SAY '          CHECK NUMBER'  GET CHECKNO
CLEAR GETS
@ 7,10 SAY  'PAID TO THE ORDER OF'  GET PAIDTO
@ 9,10 SAY  'ENTER AMOUNT OF CHECK'  GET AMOUNT
@ 11,10 SAY  'ENTER DATE (mm/dd/yy)'  GET DATE
@ 13,10 SAY  'IS THIS CHECK DEDUCTIBLE (Y/N)'  GET DEDUCT
READ
RETURN
```

Figure 12-5. Procedure for Check Entry B:CHECKENT

The command GO BOTTOM positions the DBMS to the last record in the database. This record contains the last check number used. The check number you want to enter must be the number following that one. This new check number is temporarily stored to the memory variable CNO by STORE CHECKNO+1 TO CNO. A blank record is added to the database. The new check number is written in the blank record by REPLACE CHECKNO WITH CNO.

The instruction CLEAR GETS prevents cursor movement to the fields displayed by GET commands prior to the CLEAR GETS. The display produced by this procedure is similar to Screen 12-2, except the cursor is in the leftmost character of PAIDTO and the check number is displayed. See Screen 12-3.

```
CHECK NUMBER :1250:

PAID TO THE ORDER OF :◆                                    :

ENTER AMOUNT OF CHECK :                        :

ENTER DATE (mm/dd/yy) :                          :

IS THIS CHECK DEDUCTIBLE (Y/N) : :

                          Screen 12-3
```

MENU OPTION #2

Number 2 procedure allows you to enter deposits in your electronic bankbook. Figure 12-6 illustrates the deposit entry procedure, named B:DEPOSITS.

```
APPEND BLANK
REPLACE DEPOSIT WITH Y, PAID TO WITH 'DEPOSIT'
@ 9,10 SAY 'ENTER AMOUNT OF DEPOSIT' GET AMOUNT
@ 11,10 SAY 'ENTER DATE (mm/dd/yy)' GET DATE
READ
RETURN

        Figure 12-6.  Procedure For Entering A Deposit
```

It is similar to but much simpler than B:CHECKENT — the procedure for entering checks. Screen 12-4 is the display produced by B:DEPOSITS.

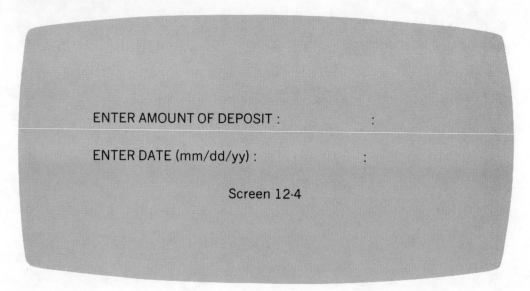

ENTER AMOUNT OF DEPOSIT :   :

ENTER DATE (mm/dd/yy) :   :

Screen 12-4

Again, the procedure is similar to APPEND except for added detail in the descriptive prompt and the fact that all fields are not displayed.

MENU OPTION #3

The third menu selection allows 'error correction' change of a previously entered record. In dBASE II, this could be accomplished with either the EDIT or BROWSE commands. As you may suspect, you can write a procedure similar to EDIT, except prompts will be descriptive text rather than fieldnames.

A procedure that will do this is shown as Figure 12-7.

```
ACCEPT 'PRESS C FOR CHECK, D FOR DEPOSIT' TO TYPE
IF TYPE='C'
    ACCEPT 'ENTER CHECK NUMBER' TO FINDER
    FIND &FINDER
    ERASE
    @ 5,10 SAY '        CHECK NUMBER' GET CHECKNO
    CLEAR GETS
    @ 7,10 SAY 'PAID TO THE ORDER OF' GET PAIDTO
    @ 9,10 SAY 'ENTER AMOUNT OF CHECK' GET AMOUNT
    @ 11,10 SAY 'ENTER DATE (mm/dd/yy)' GET DATE
    @ 13,10 SAY 'IS THIS CHECK DEDUCTIBLE (Y/N)' GET DEDUCT
    READ
ENDIF
IF TYPE='D'
    ACCEPT 'ENTER DATE OF DEPOSIT' TO FINDER
    DISPLAY FOR DEPOSIT.AND.DATE=FINDER
    INPUT 'ENTER RECORD NUMBER TO BE EDITED' TO FINDER
    GOTO FINDER
    ERASE
    @ 9,10 SAY 'ENTER AMOUNT OF DEPOSIT' GET AMOUNT
    @ 11,10 SAY 'ENTER DATE (mm/dd/yy)' GET DATE
    READ
ENDIF
RETURN
```

Figure 12-7. A Procedure For Changing A Record

Our first problem is how to find the record we want. If we want to change a check entry this is pretty simple — we have the computer find the record containing the check number for the check entry we want to change. If we have a deposit, however, we have to find the record some other way, because there is no check number field entry when entering a deposit.

In our example database there is no unique deposit record identification (except, of course, for the record number). This exemplifies the need to plan. Our lack of planning leads us to seek a work-a-round solution. It is tempting to use the date as our change criteria. Unfortunately, even if we never have more than one deposit per day, we can err when entering a deposit such that there are two deposit entries per day. The solution is use of the record number as the criteria. Displaying all records for a particular date enables access to the appropriate record number.

The procedure has two sections, selected according to whether or not the record we wish to change was a check:

(1) If it is a check we find the record containing the desired check number and then produce the same display we used to enter data into a check record. The record is found by the FIND command and the memory variable FINDER. FIND &FINDER means to find the record corresponding to the check number stored in finder. The ampersand tells the computer that FINDER is a memory variable.

(2) The second section deals with the need to change a deposit record, not a check record. The computer first asks for the date of interest, displays the deposit records for that date, and then asks for the record number of the deposit record to be changed. GOTO FINDER positions the database to the record with the record number stored in FINDER. The change display is the same display used to enter information into a deposit record.

MENU OPTION #4

The fourth menu item provides for looking at the check register contents, to determine whether or not you wrote a particular check. Figure 12-8 is a simple procedure providing a cursory 'look through' capability.

```
USE B:CHECKREG
ACCEPT 'ENTER MONTH AND YEAR (mm/yy)' TO TIME
DISPLAY FOR $(DATE,1,2)+$(DATE,7,2)=$(TIME,1,2)+$(TIME,4,2)
USE B:CHECKREG INDEX B:CHECKNO
WAIT
RETURN
```

Figure 12-8. A Procedure To Look Through The Check Register

This procedure provides display of all records from a particular month. In this case we use the database without the index file, because the index file seems to separate the deposit records and check records and we would ordinarily want to see them displayed together in time sequence.

The procedure displays (in record order) the records for a designated month and year. The records are displayed 15 at a time (this is the way DISPLAY works). After the fifteenth record is displayed, the word WAITING will appear. Pressing any key except SHIFT or CONTROL causes display of the next fifteen records. In the field DATE, the first and second characters indicate the month while the 7th and 8th indicate the year. In the memory variable TIME, the first and second characters indicate the month while the 4th and 5th indicate the year.

The DISPLAY instruction compares the 1st, 2nd, 7th, and 8th characters of DATE with the 1st, 2nd, 4th, and 5th characters of TIME. When these two sets of characters match the record will be displayed.

When the procedure is complete, the indexed file is again selected for use.

This menu item is a good candidate for a 2nd menu, although we will not include one here. The second menu would include a selection of possible displays, in many cases the kind of REPORTS used in the liquor store inventory example of Chapter II.

MENU OPTION #5

Menu item 5 — listing deductible checks — allows the opportunity to use a REPORT FORM within a command file. Figure 12-8A shows the deductible check listing procedure.

```
ACCEPT 'DO YOU WANT A PRINTED COPY (Y/N)' TO QUERY
IF QUERY='Y'
    REPORT FORM B:DEDUCT TO PRINT FOR DEDUCT
ENDIF
IF QUERY='N'
    REPORT FORM B:DEDUCT FOR DEDUCT
ENDIF
RETURN
```

Figure 12-8A

The resulting report is shown as Figure 12-8B. Reports are a convenient way to display data.

```
PAGE NO. 00001
02/01/82

                                        DEDUCTIBLE EXPENSES
    CHECK
      NO          PAID TO              DATE           AMOUNT

    208      WRACKING PAIN HOSP      6/22/81            98.50
    227      QP COMPUTERS            8/14/81          4011.04
    234      DR DENTAL,DDS (KEN)     8/21/81            91.00
    267      QP COMPUTERS           10/24/81           486.38
    289      COMPUTE-AWHILE         11/27/81            79.50
    323      LEMON MICRO            01/23/82          1257.16
    324      QP ELECTRONICS         01/23/82           344.50

  ** TOTAL **                                         6368.08


                        Figure 12-8B
```

MENU OPTION #6

Menu item (6) determines the current account balance. This procedure is nearly identical to B:BALANCE developed in the previous chapter. Figure 12-9 shows this variation.

```
USE B:CHECKREG
STORE 0 TO MDEPOSIT, CHECKS
DO WHILE .NOT.EOF
   IF DEPOSIT
      STORE AMOUNT+MDEPOSIT TO MDEPOSIT
   ENDIF
   IF .NOT.DEPOSIT
      STORE AMOUNT+CHECKS TO CHECKS
   ENDIF
SKIP
ENDDO
@ 5,15 SAY 'TOTAL DEPOSITS'  GET MDEPOSIT
@ 7,15 SAY 'TOTAL CHECKS'  GET CHECKS
STORE MDEPOSIT-CHECKS TO BALANCE
@ 9,15 SAY 'BALANCE        '  GET BALANCE
CLEAR GETS
WAIT
USE B:CHECKREG INDEX B:CHECKNO
RETURN
```

Figure 12-9. Procedure To Calculate The Current Account Balance

Here we use the dBASE @ command to display as shown in Screen 12-5. Another difference from the original B:BALANCE is the use of the RETURN command instead of the CANCEL command.

```
          TOTAL DEPOSITS :      10677.80:

          TOTAL CHECKS   :       9450.51:

          BALANCE        :       1227.29:

WAITING ◆
```

Screen 12-5

Because it takes less time to calculate the balance using the unindexed B:CHECKREG, we do not use the indexed database for this procedure. This time efficiency results from reading the records sequentially, instead of jumping back and forth according to the index. An indexed database requires movement back and forth and the disk read head must also move back and forth.

MENU OPTION #7

The seventh menu entry checks up on the bank. You need a way to monitor how well the bank is taking care of your account. This procedure is one way to do that.

Balancing a checking account is sometimes called reconciliation. Whatever it's called, it always consists of four parts:

(1)   Checking off canceled checks

(2)   Checking off canceled deposits

(3)   Entering bank charges

(4)   Take your final balance
      add outstanding checks
      subtract outstanding deposits
      compare the result to the bank's balance

The procedure to 'reconcile' your account is shown in Figure 12-10. This procedure is also a menu, allowing you to undertake each of the four parts and deal with it until you are satisfied.

```
STORE ' ' TO CHOICE
DO WHILE .NOT.CHOICE='5'
ERASE
@ 5,15 SAY '(1) Check off canceled checks'
@ 7,15 SAY '(2) Check off canceled deposits'
@ 9,15 SAY '(3) Enter bank charges'
@ 11,15 SAY '(4) Compare Bank Balance to Your Balance'
@ 13,15 SAY '(5) Return to the Main Menu'
@ 20,15 SAY 'ENTER YOUR SELECTION' GET CHOICE
READ
DO CASE
CASE CHOICE='1'
    DO B:BALMENU1
CASE CHOICE='2'
    DO B:BALMENU2
CASE CHOICE='3'
    DO B:BALMENU3
CASE CHOICE='4'
    DO B:BALMENU4
ENDCASE
ENDDO
RETURN
```

Figure 12-10. A Menu Procedure To Balance A Checkbook

If you compare this menu with the main check register menu you find a few differences. These differences illustrate the concept that you can often accomplish the same result in different ways.

DO WHILE T is replaced by DO WHILE .NOT.CHOICE='5'. Entering 5 terminates the do loop and returns you to the first (main) menu. Selection of a character which is not a menu choice will redisplay the menu.

A new command, 'DO CASE' is introduced in this example. Similar in concept to IF, DO CASE is often used where there are a number of choices for action and the choices are exclusive. Only one of the possible cases is acted on — even if several apply. The first case to satisfy the condition is acted on. In a string of IFs it is possible that more than one would satisfy some condition and be acted on — even if it is undesirable.

This particular menu procedure construction is preferable to that used for the main menu example. Choice of a procedure name allows easy identification of that specific procedure should you come across the name in some other context.

CHECKING OFF CANCELLED CHECKS

The first menu item allows 'cancellation' of checks that have cleared the bank. In the example procedure, shown in Figure 12-11, the check record is found and the pertinent data displayed on the screen as a 'check.' If the record displayed is the one you want you 'cancel' the record. A representative display from this procedure is shown in Screen 12-6.

```
STORE ' ' TO ENABLE
STORE 0 TO NUMBER,TOTAL
DO WHILE .NOT.ENABLE='X'
   ERASE
   STORE '        ' GET FINDER
   @ 5,10 SAY 'ENTER CHECK NUMBER' TO FINDER
   READ
   FIND &FINDER
   @ 7,10 SAY 'CHECK PAID TO' GET PAIDTO
   @ 9,10 SAY 'THE AMOUNT IS' GET AMOUNT
   @ 7,50 SAY 'DATED' GET DATE
   CLEAR GETS
   @ 9,50 SAY 'CANCEL (Y/N)' GET CANCEL
   READ
   IF CANCEL
      STORE TOTAL+AMOUNT TO TOTAL
      STORE NUMBER+1 TO NUMBER
      @ 12,10 SAY 'NUMBER OF CHECKS CANCELED' GET NUMBER
      @ 12,40 SAY 'TOTALING' GET TOTAL
   ENDIF
   CLEAR GETS
   @ 15,10 SAY 'ENTER X WHEN FINISHED—RETURN TO CONTINUE' GET ENABLE
   READ
ENDDO
RETURN
```

Figure 12-11. A Procedure For 'Cancelling Checks'

ENTER CHECK NUMBER :1221:

CHECK PAID TO :TELEPHONE COMPANY   :   DATED :11/29/81:

THE AMOUNT IS :   34.56:   CANCEL (Y/N) :Y:

NUMBER OF CHECKS CANCELED :   34:   TOTALING : 574.66:

ENTER X WHEN FINISHED — RETURN TO CONTINUE : ♦ :

Screen 12-6

When you have finished entering cancelled checks the number of checks cancelled and their total value should agree with the bank's statement. If not you need to determine why they do not agree. The procedure can be repeated if necessary.

CHECKING OFF CANCELLED DEPOSITS

Having completed the check cancelling procedure you move on to deposit 'cancelling.' The procedure to accomplish this is B:BALMENU2 and is shown in Figure 12-12.

```
STORE T TO ENABLE
STORE 0 TO NR,DEP
DO WHILE ENABLE
    ERASE
    REMARK WHEN FINISHED ENTER — STOP — FOR THE RECORD NUMBER
    REMARK
    DISPLAY AMOUNT,DATE FOR DEPOSIT.AND..NOT.CANCEL
    ACCEPT 'ENTER RECORD NUMBER TO BE CANCELED' TO F1
        IF F1='STOP'
        STORE F TO ENABLE
        ELSE
            STORE VAL(F1) TO FINDER
            GOTO FINDER
            STORE NR+1 TO NR
            STORE DEP+AMOUNT TO DEP
            REPLACE CANCEL WITH Y
        ENDIF
ENDDO
    ERASE
    @ 10,10 SAY 'NUMBER OF CANCELED DEPOSITS'  GET NR
    @ 15,10 SAY 'TOTAL VALUE WAS'  GET DEP
    WAIT
    RETURN
```

Figure 12-12. A Procedure To 'Cancel' Deposits

In this example we 'turn off' the do loop from within the procedure. This loop operates as long as the memory variable ENABLE is true. Note that the T and F do not need to be enclosed in delimiters. Because the computer 'assumes' them to be LOGICAL values. T stands for true and F for false.

Note also that the record number was stored as a character set. (ACCEPT is a way to tell the computer the data entered are characters). If we use INPUT we can not enter the word 'STOP' into the memory variable F1. By the way, it is not a good idea to use T or F as memory variable names. It is a source of possible computer confusion in some circumstances. In this case, if we use F instead of F1, the statement STORE F TO ENABLE would be ambiguous. Which 'F' — false, or the contents of F?

Since we stored the record number as a character string we need to convert it back to a number if we are to use the command GOTO. Accomplish this with the command STORE VAL(F1) TO FINDER. This means store the value of F1 to the memory variable FINDER. As you might expect, numbers can be converted to characters and numbers stored as characters can be converted back to numbers.

ENTERING BANK CHARGES

The third procedure in this menu allows you to enter bank charges into the database. The procedure for accomplishing this is shown as Figure 12-13.

```
ERASE
APPEND BLANK
@ 5,5 SAY 'ENTER BANK CHARGES' GET AMOUNT
@ 7,5 SAY 'ENTER DATE (mm/dd/yy)' GET DATE
READ
REPL DEPOSIT WITH N, PAIDTO WITH 'BANK CHARGE', CANCEL WITH Y
RETURN
```

Figure 12-13. A Procedure To Enter Bank Charges

Note that the charges were treated as checks so the arithmetic works correctly. Charges and checks are both debits against the account. Charges are also 'cancelled' at the time of entry, because they are a part of the statement.

Many banks today also offer interest paying checking accounts. Because of this a 'real' check register menu should also include an entry for bank credits.

Menu item 4 provides for comparison of your version of the account balance to the bank's conclusion. A procedure to accomplish this is shown as Figure 12-14.

```
ERASE
INPUT 'ENTER BANKS VERSION OF BALANCE' TO BANKBAL
SUM AMOUNT TO SPENT FOR CANCEL.AND..NOT.DEPOSIT
SUM AMOUNT TO EARNED FOR CANCEL.AND.DEPOSIT
STORE EARNED—SPENT TO MYBALANCE
@ 10,10 SAY 'MY VERSION OF BALANCE' GET MYBALANCE
STORE BANKBAL—MYBALANCE TO ERROR
@ 15,10 SAY 'THE BANKS ERROR IS' GET ERROR
CLEAR GETS
WAIT
RETURN
```

Figure 12-14. Procedure For Monthly Balancing

In this example we did not need to consider outstanding checks and deposits. You do this normally in a 'paper' checkbook because of the 'running balance.' In the computer checkbook we ignore outstanding entries and work, hopefully, with the same set of data the bank uses. If all of the data is entered correctly the resulting display should be like that shown in Screen 12-7.

ENTER BANKS VERSION OF BALANCE: 1227.29

MY VERSION OF BALANCE   :1227.29:

THE BANKS ERROR IS :   0:

WAITING ♦

Screen 12-7

In this chapter we have attempted to describe a complete database system for maintaining a check register. Some details were overlooked in the interest of describing the basic concepts involved. The menu system is a convenient way of using the computer for routine tasks to be accomplished on a daily, weekly, or other periodic basis. The menu may contain sub-menus for the more complex tasks. As a rule, one would expect that the more frequently used menu items would be on the 'highest' menus and that those least frequently used would be on the 'lowest' menus.

CHAPTER XIII

PROCEDURES TO MINIMIZE
ERROR & TEDIUM

The usefulness of your database depends heavily on data content accuracy. Data is normally entered by people and people make mistakes. Earlier in this book we discussed briefly using computer aids for faster, less tedious data entry. There is often a temptation to emphasize the 'quicker' and worry little about the 'tedious.' Presumably, the idea is to reduce the cost of entering the data. Unfortunately, any apparent 'economy' is often false.

Computer aids are only valuable when they increase entry potential without increasing errors. Most data entry errors are either typographical (which is self-explanatory) or clerical, where the eye shifts a line while transferring data from paper to the computer.

Typographical errors are often (but not always) nuisance errors. 'Scotch' might be entered as 'scitch'. Menus are sometimes used to avoid such spelling errors. The problem: press the wrong menu selection and you end up entering 'whiskey' instead of 'scotch.' This is much more serious than a simple spelling error. You can install a check for this kind of error:

LIQUOR SELECTION WAS SCOTCH
CORRECT (Y/N)

Now, this is nice, but this bit of nonsense takes more time (and trouble) than typing in 'scotch' in the first place.

You want data entry to go quickly. But, more importantly, you want it to go smoothly and accurately. A pleasant working environment will do far more to ensure rapid, accurate data entry than a lot of 'clever' gimmicks.

Procedures to Minimize
Error and Tedium

Nevertheless, many data entry tasks are truly routine. It is reasonable to automate these if possible in order to reduce tedium and to provide protection against available error.

The easiest error to protect against is entry of 'impossible data'. In an error of this sort, the data entered falls outside of a range of permitted values. For example, if you are entering student data for an elementary school, there are only so many rooms a student can be assigned to. The computer can thus protect against entering a 'not allowed' room number. It can't protect you against accidentally entering a legitimate (but incorrect) room number.

How do you protect against 'impossible data' entry? It isn't exactly trivial but it is pretty easy. Let's suppose we have a little procedure to enter a student's name, room number, and grade into a database. To keep this simple our school only goes through the third grade and has but four rooms — 101,102,103, and 104. Our sample procedure (without error checking) might look like that shown in Figure 13-1.

```
APPEND BLANK
ERASE
@ 10,10 SAY 'ENTER STUDENTS NAME' GET NAME
@ 12,10 SAY 'ROOM NUMBER' GET ROOM
@ 12,40 SAY 'GRADE' GET GRADE
READ
RETURN


                    Figure 13-1
```

If we add error checks it could look like that shown in Figure 13-2.

218

```
APPEND BLANK
ERASE
@ 10,10 SAY 'ENTER STUDENTS NAME' GET NAME
@ 12,10 SAY 'ROOM NUMBER' GET ROOM
@ 12,40 SAY 'GRADE' GET GRADE
READ
IF .NOT.(ROOM='101'.OR.ROOM='102'.OR.ROOM='103'.OR.ROOM='104')
ERASE
@ 12,10 SAY 'YOU HAVE ACCIDENTLY ENTERED AN INCORRECT ROOM
   NUMBER'
@ 14,10 SAY 'PLEASE ENTER THE CORRECT ROOM' GET ROOM
READ
ENDIF
IF .NOT.(GRADE='K'.OR.GRADE='1'.OR.GRADE='2'.OR.GRADE='3')
ERASE
@ 12,10 SAY 'YOU HAVE ACCIDENTLY ENTERED AN INCORRECT GRADE'
@ 14,10 SAY 'PLEASE ENTER THE CORRECT GRADE' GET GRADE
READ
ENDIF
RETURN
```

Figure 13-2

Note the structure of the logic lines. This is the correct way to set up logic when you don't want one of several possible entries for a field. These could also have been set up as

```
IF .NOT.ROOM$'101,102,103,104'
IF .NOT.GRADE$'K,1,2,3'
```

These would have obtained identical results.

If you feel there is a reasonable chance the entry still won't be correct even with this 'second chance', you can use a 'DO' loop instead of the IF.

```
DO WHILE .NOT.(ROOM='101'.OR.ROOM='102'.OR.ROOM='103'.OR.ROOM='104')
ERASE
@ 12,10 SAY 'YOU HAVE ACCIDENTLY ENTERED AN INCORRECT ROOM
    NUMBER'
@ 14,10 SAY 'PLEASE ENTER THE CORRECT ROOM' GET ROOM
READ
ENDDO
DO WHILE .NOT.(GRADE='K'.OR.GRADE='1'.OR.GRADE='2'.OR.GRADE='3')
ERASE
@ 12,10 SAY 'YOU HAVE ACCIDENTLY ENTERED AN INCORRECT GRADE'
@ 14,10 SAY 'PLEASE ENTER THE CORRECT GRADE' GET GRADE
READ
ENDDO
```

When you USE a 'DO' loop, you can't go any further until you get it right.

A very pragmatic example of a field needing protection is the DATE field, from the check register examples of the last chapter. In our examples we entered the date each and every time we entered a check or a deposit. Now that really is a nuisance — especially if you write a lot of checks. In addition, we wanted to 'see' check displays based on the date.

Entering the date less often is one very straightforward way to reduce the chance for error. In this particular example, we could enter the date once when we select the procedure B:BANKMENU. This is done by storing the date into a memory variable, and using the REPLACE command to write the date into the DATE field.

A neat alternative to this approach is to use the 'date' entered when you chose dBASE. This date can be entered into the date field by

```
REPLACE DATE WITH DATE()
```

When you entered the dBASE date it was stored in memory location DATE( ). It is the same as the 'date of last change' in your database structure.

DATE( ) takes eight character spaces as does the DATE field in our example. Using all eight characters each time you enter a date is very important. We didn't want to make a big deal about this in the last chapter. There were other important things in that chapter. We want to make a big deal about the date in this chapter.

First of all, while you know that

2/12/80 is the same as 02/12/80

the computer doesn't. It just compares characters on a space by space basis.

```
 1  2  3  4  5  6  7  8
_____

 2  /  1  2  /  8  0
 0  2  /  1  2  /  8  0
```

Because character fields are left justified, character fields such as this one begin comparison with the leftmost character. As you can see from a space by space comparison, there is no comparison. For a lot of data this kind of 'problem' might not be a concern. In this case, however, you might want to use DATE as a key for displaying data. In that case it is very important to have a consistent manner of entering the characters.

If there is some possibility of improper data entry and the date is important for 'ordering' the records, there are several ways the computer can help you to enter the data properly. One possiblity is use of dBASE II's PICTURE command. Instead of having the instruction read

@ 10,15 SAY 'ENTER THE DATE' GET DATE

use

@ 10,15 SAY 'ENTER THE DATE' GET DATE PICTURE '99/99/99'

As the computer does the procedure, it will display

ENTER THE DATE :   / / :

The '/' separators are fixed into the display. When you enter the numbers for the date the computer skips over the /'s. As an added benefit, the computer accepts only numbers into the spaces occupied by the 9's. This doesn't entirely eliminate the possibility of problems — but it helps, and it does make data entry easier.

How can we be sure the date is always entered in the proper manner — with or without the PICTURE command? It turns out we can easily accomplish this trick with a procedure using the positions of the characters in the field. We touched on this idea in the last chapter. Now we'll go over it in a bit of detail. It's not difficult, and it's invaluable.

The third and sixth characters are supposed to be /'s. We can guarantee they will be with the use of PICTURE. But even without PICTURE, we can put the date together the way it needs to be.

```
1  2  3  4  5  6  7  8
_____

m  m  /  d  d  /  y  y        should be

m  /  d  /  y  y              could be
```

There are a number of possibilities for 'could be.' A simple (if lengthy) procedure to make any legitimate 'could be' into what it 'should be' is shown in Figure 13-3.

```
IF .NOT.$(DATE,3,1)='/'          (if the third character doesn't = /
   STORE '0'+DATE TO DATE        adds a 0 to the beginning of
ENDIF                            DATE it's now all right or the
                                 'day' isn't this means that 'day'
                                 is less than 10.)

IF .NOT.$(DATE,6,1)='/'          (if the 6th character isn't a /)
   STORE $(DATE,1,3)+'0'+$(DATE,5,4)
   TO DATE
ENDIF
```

Figure 13-3

222

This simple little procedure will make sure that the date is arranged as we want it.

mm/dd/yy

There is a new ingredient in this procedure. An example is:

$(DATE,1,3)

This means 'the first three characters in the field DATE.' The first number means the position of the starting character. The second number is the number of characters. This example shows us we can manipulate characters if we want to, which is often quite useful.

As a further example, let's suppose we want to index the contents of our check register database by date. When we arrange items by date we use

yy/mm/dd

We usually don't think a lot about this — but that's the way we would sort items by date. On the other hand we usually use

mm/dd/yy

as the way of entering dates, to get the computer to arrange items by date in the same way we would need to use the field position. The data can be properly arranged by

INDEX ON $(DATE,7,2)+$(1,5) TO B:DATE

The index file B:DATE allows us to access data records in order of the date.

We needed to manipulate the date because our way of reading dates is not easily usable for the computer. It 'orders' character strings starting from the leftmost character. The three dates

04/22/81
03/21/82
01/22/82

would be 'ordered' as

01/22/82
03/21/82
04/22/81

without instructing the computer otherwise — as in the example above. The sample index instruction would properly arrange the dates as

04/22/81
01/22/82
03/21/82

The computer is always precise and literal. It can only work correctly with exact contents. We are associative — that is, we know that Bob Byers and Robert Byers and Robert A. Byers are the same person. The computer can't know that. It works with comparisons. There are times when we can become frustrated by this. On the other hand, this means the computer is always predictable. The rules are fixed and precise. Once we accept those rules, we can easily obtain profitable help from the computer.

CHAPTER XIV

SPECIAL REPORTS

You can use procedures to prepare special reports in just about any format you might desire. Procedures can be used to prepare reports that cannot normally be obtained from the DBMS's Report Writer. It may take a little more effort than is required to obtain a report from the database system's Report Writer (dBASE II's REPORT command). The result may well be worth the extra effort since it produces a report exactly as you want it.

To illustrate the use of procedures to prepare special reports we will work through an example of a typical report that cannot easily be accommodated by the standard report writer.

An elementary school uses a microcomputer with a database management system for student record keeping. At the beginning of the school year, and periodically thereafter, it is desirable to provide copies of class lists to staff members such as the school nurse, the librarian, the school secretary, and the classroom teacher.

The school database contains, among other items, fields which record each student's progress in reading and mathematics, room number, grade, teacher's name, whether or not the student was retained in grade. The relevent parts of the database structure are shown in Figure 14-1.

FIELDNAME	FIELDTYPE	WIDTH
NAME	C	30
ROOM	C	3
GRADE	C	1
TEACHER	C	15
RETAINED	L	1
READING	N	2
MATH	N	2
SEX	C	1

Figure 14-1. School Database Structure (Partial)

The school wants to print and distribute class rosters which look like the one shown in Figure 14-2.

```
                       SPECTACULAR SCHOOL


TEACHER: WISEMAN                    9 SEPTEMBER 1982
ROOM:    101
GRADE:   6

              CLASS ROSTER FOR THE 1982/1983 SCHOOL YEAR
```

NAME	READING	MATH	
Aardvark, Anthony	21	88	
Anerson, Hann	43	29	
Apple, Wise	87	29	RETAINED
.	.	.	
.	.	.	
Zachary, Abram	34	19	

```
CLASS SIZE: 28
BOYS:      14
GIRLS:     14


READING AVERAGE: 43.32
MATH AVERAGE:    62.67
```

Figure 14-2. Example Of Special Report

This particular example cannot be prepared (at least in this format) using dBASE II's standard report writer. The bulk of the report can be handled by REPORT of course. It is the special annotation of

TEACHER
ROOM
GRADE
CLASS SIZE
BOYS
GIRLS
READING AVERAGE
MATH AVERAGE

that cannot be readily accommodated in this format.

```
SET TALK OFF
USE B:SCHOOL
INDEX ON GRADE+ROOM+NAME TO B:ROSTER
USE B:SCHOOL INDEX B:ROSTER
ACCEPT 'ENTER THE DATE' TO DATE
SET PRINT ON
DO WHILE .NOT.EOF
   ?
   ?
   ?
   ?
   ?
   ? '                              SPECTACULAR SCHOOL'
   ?
   ? '          TEACHER: ',TEACHER,'                    ',DATE
   ? '          ROOM:    ',ROOM
   ? '          GRADE:   ',GRADE
   ?
   ?'          CLASS ROSTER FOR THE 1982/1983 SCHOOL YEAR'
   ?'          _____',
   ?'            NAME          READING          MATH'
   ?'          _____',
   ?
   STORE ROOM TO MROOM
   STORE GRADE TO MGRADE
   STORE 0 TO BOYS,GIRLS,XREADING,XMATH
DO WHILE ROOM=MROOM.AND.GRADE=MGRADE.AND..NOT.EOF
 STORE '    ' TO RET
  IF RETAINED
    STORE 'RETAINED' TO RET
  ENDIF
 ? '         ',NAME,'         ',READING,'        ',MATH,'        ',RET
  IF SEX='M'
    STORE BOYS+1 TO BOYS
   else
    STORE GIRLS+1 TO GIRLS
  ENDIF
  STORE XREADING+READING TO XREADING
  STORE XMATH+MATH TO XMATH
  SKIP
ENDDO
```

```
?
? '            CLASS SIZE:',STR(BOYS+GIRLS,2)
? '            BOYS:      ',STR(BOYS,2)
? '            GIRLS:      ',STR(GIRLS,2)
?
? '            READING AVERAGE:',STR(XREADING/(BOYS+GIRLS),6,2)
? '            MATH AVERAGE:    ',STR(XMATH/(BOYS+GIRLS),6,2)
   EJECT
ENDDO
SET PRINT OFF
SET TALK ON
CANCEL
```

This procedure will provide a set of printed reports with each class roster printed on a separate page. It is completely tailored to the needs and desires of the people who want it. In the following paragraphs we will go over this procedure and describe each step in some detail.

To accomplish this we will start out with the basic element of this procedure. Then we will add new elements and continue to iterate until we arrive at the final procedure. At each iteration we will add the new (or changed) statements in bold faced type. The most basic element is a do loop that produces a continuous listing of all of the students in the school (this is nothing more than a 'procedural' version of the command LIST).

```
                    SET TALK OFF
                    DO WHILE .NOT. EOF
                      DISPLAY
                      SKIP
                    ENDDO
                    SET TALK ON
                    CANCEL
```

Figure 14-3. Procedural Version of dBASE II Command LIST

SET TALK OFF/ON

Nearly all procedures will begin and end with this command. When working from the keyboard it is desireable for the computer to respond (talk) to you each time you issue a command. This is not true when using procedures. You will wish to inhibit the computer from 'talking' except when you want it to. In this case we want to see the record contents (DISPLAY) but we don't want to have the computer echo the record number from the command SKIP.

SKIP

This command will advance the database one record each time it is used. If we had not SET TALK OFF, the computer would display the record number each time SKIP was used.

If SKIP is used with a database that is not indexed, the records will be advanced in the order of the record numbers. If an indexed database is used, the records will be advanced in their 'logical' order.

DO WHILE .NOT. EOF

Tells the computer to repeat the commands DISPLAY and SKIP until the end of the database file is reached.

In our next step of explaining the example special report procedure we will:

Tell the computer which database file to use

INDEX the database by class

Tell the computer to use the indexed database

Display only the fields that we desire

```
SET TALK OFF
USE B:SCHOOL
INDEX ON GRADE+ROOM+NAME TO B:ROSTER
USE B:SCHOOL INDEX B:ROSTER
DO WHILE .NOT. EOF
   ? NAME,READING,MATH
  SKIP
ENDDO
SET TALK ON
CANCEL
```

Figure 14-4. Modified Procedural Version of dBASE II Command LIST

This procedure now produces a screen display with the students displayed alphabetically by grade and room. The DISPLAY command was replaced by the ?. This prevents the record number from being displayed and requires less typing than DISPLAY OFF which would accomplish the same result. Only the contents of the fields NAME, READING, and MATH will be displayed.

For our next step we will add the commands to produce a simple printout of the class rosters. At this step in our development of this procedure, the resulting printout would be very crude. Each class roster would be just a list of student name, reading level and math level — beginning at the very top of the page. There would not be any left margin.

```
SET TALK OFF
USE B:SCHOOL
INDEX ON GRADE+ROOM+NAME TO B:ROSTER
USE B:SCHOOL INDEX B:ROSTER
SET PRINT ON
DO WHILE .NOT. EOF
    STORE ROOM TO MROOM
    STORE GRADE TO MGRADE
    DO WHILE ROOM=MROOM.AND.GRADE='MGRADE'.AND..NOT.EOF
    ? NAME,READING,MATH
    SKIP
    ENDDO
    EJECT
ENDDO
SET PRINT OFF
SET TALK ON
CANCEL
```

Figure 14-5. Elementary Version Of Class Roster Procedure

SET PRINT ON/OFF

This turns the printer on and off. You should usually turn the printer on after you SET TALK OFF. Similarly, turn the printer off before you SET TALK ON.

STORE ROOM TO MROOM
STORE GRADE TO MGRADE

These two commands allow you to set up the DO LOOP for listing each class separately. They allow the computer to automatically establish the beginning and end of a class grouping.

DO WHILE ROOM=MROOM.AND.GRADE=MGRADE.AND..NOT.EOF

Here we have a DO LOOP within a DO LOOP. The inner DO LOOP is fully contained within the outer loop. As long as each record meets the conditions:

The room number is the same as MROOM

The grade is the same as MGRADE

The end of file is not encountered

The procedure will continue to print out each student name, reading level, and math level. Note the double period between AND and NOT. This is the correct way to enter the condition.

EJECT

This causes the printer paper to be advanced to the next sheet.

This procedure is relatively straightforward. The outer loop allows the entire database to be listed. Once we enter the outer loop (DO WHILE .NOT. EOF) the room and grade of the first record will be stored to the memory variables MROOM and MGRADE. Then we enter the inner loop. This inner loop will be repeated until the database is advanced to a record where ROOM and GRADE do not equal the contents of the memory variables MROOM and MGRADE. When this occurs the paper is ejected and we go back to the beginning of the outer loop — store the new room and grade to the memory variables and continue. If we encounter the end of file marker, we turn the printer off and we are through. Note that the inner loop also has .NOT. EOF as a part of its condition.

At this point we are ready to add the commands that perform the actions necessary to:

Count the boys
Count the girls
Add the contents of the reading and math fields for each class

```
        SET TALK OFF
        USE B:SCHOOL
        INDEX ON GRADE+ROOM+NAME TO B:ROSTER
        USE B:SCHOOL INDEX B:ROSTER
        SET PRINT ON
        DO WHILE .NOT.EOF
           STORE ROOM TO MROOM
           STORE GRADE TO MGRADE
           STORE 0 TO BOYS,GIRLS, XREADING,XMATH
        DO WHILE ROOM=MROOM.AND.GRADE=MGRADE.AND..NOT.EOF
          ? '           ',NAME,READING,MATH
         IF SEX='M'
           STORE BOYS+1 TO BOYS
         ELSE
           STORE GIRLS+1 TO GIRLS
         ENDIF
         STORE XREADING+READING TO XREADING
         STORE XMATH+MATH TO XMATH
         SKIP
        ENDDO
         EJECT
        ENDDO
        SET PRINT OFF
        SET TALK ON
        CANCEL
```

Figure 14-6

STORE 0 TO BOYS,GIRLS,XREADING,XMATH

This command creates four memory variables

BOYS
GIRLS
XREADING
XMATH

and sets their initial values to zero.

```
IF SEX='M'
    STORE BOYS+1 TO BOYS
ELSE
    STORE GIRLS+1 TO GIRLS
ENDIF
```

In the inner loop we increment the value of BOYS by one if the content of SEX is M. Otherwise we increment GIRLS by one.

```
STORE XREADING+READING TO XREADING
STORE XMATH+MATH TO XMATH
```

In addition we add the contents of the reading field to the memory variable XREADING and the contents of the math field to the memory variable XMATH.

At this point we now have set up the procedure to be able to print the specially formatted information at the bottom of each class roster.

```
CLASS SIZE
BOYS
GIRLS
READING AVERAGE
MATH AVERAGE
```

This is accomplished by the commands:

```
?
? '            CLASS SIZE:',STR(BOYS+GIRLS,2)
? '            BOYS:      ',STR(BOYS,2)
? '            GIRLS:     ',STR(GIRLS,2)
?
? '            READING AVERAGE:',STR(XREADING/(BOYS+GIRLS),6,2)
? '            MATH AVERAGE:    ',STR(XMATH/(BOYS+GIRLS),6,2)
```

The question mark (?) when used alone will produce a blank line on the screen and/or the printer. The command line

```
? '            CLASS SIZE: ',STR(BOYS+GIRLS,2)
```

will produce a printed line which looks like the one shown in the example. The starting blank spaces within the delimiters are to provide a left margin. Without these spaces the word CLASS would begin at the left edge of the paper.

STR(BOYS+GIRLS,2)

This part of the command will take the sum of the memory variables BOYS and GIRLS and print the result as a two digit character string. In this case we know that the result cannot contain more than two characters. If we were to just use the command line as:

? '   CLASS SIZE:',BOYS+GIRLS

The sum would be printed as a ten digit field. This would put 8 blank spaces between the text 'CLASS SIZE' and the printed sum.

? '   READING AVERAGE:',STR(XREADING/(BOYS+GIRLS),6,2)

This particular version of the command is similar except that the ',2' tells the computer that we want two decimals displayed.

Now we are ready to add the commands to print the page heading and properly format the page.

```
SET TALK OFF
USE B:SCHOOL
INDEX ON GRADE+ROOM+NAME TO B:ROSTER
USE B:SCHOOL INDEX B:ROSTER
ACCEPT 'ENTER THE DATE' TO DATE
SET PRINT ON
DO WHILE .NOT.EOF
   ?
   ?
   ?
   ?
   ?
   ? '                              SPECTACULAR SCHOOL'
   ?
   ? '          TEACHER: ',TEACHER,'                        ',DATE
   ? '          ROOM:    ',ROOM
   ? '          GRADE:   ',GRADE
   ?
   ?'          CLASS ROSTER FOR THE 1982/1983 SCHOOL YEAR',
   ?'_____
   ?'          NAME           READING         MATH'          ,
   ?'_____
   ?
   STORE ROOM TO MROOM
   STORE GRADE TO MGRADE
   STORE 0 TO BOYS,GIRLS,XREADING,XMATH
DO WHILE ROOM=MROOM.AND.GRADE=MGRADE.AND..NOT.EOF
 STORE '    ' TO RET
   IF RETAINED
     STORE 'RETAINED' TO RET
   ENDIF
 ? '          ',NAME,READING,MATH,'        ',RET
 IF SEX='M'
     STORE BOYS+1 TO BOYS
    else
     STORE GIRLS+1 TO GIRLS
   ENDIF
   STORE XREADING+READING TO XREADING
   STORE XMATH+MATH TO XMATH
   SKIP
ENDDO
```

(continued on next page)

```
    ?
    ? '            CLASS SIZE:',STR(BOYS+GIRLS,2)
    ? '            BOYS:     ',STR(BOYS,2)
    ? '            GIRLS:    ',STR(GIRLS,2)
    ?
    ? '            READING AVERAGE:',STR(XREADING/(BOYS+GIRLS),6,2)
    ? '            MATH AVERAGE:    ',STR(XMATH/(BOYS+GIRLS),6,2)
  EJECT
ENDDO
SET PRINT OFF
SET TALK ON
CANCEL
```

Figure 14-7

ACCEPT 'ENTER THE DATE' TO DATE

This command allows us to enter the date in any form that we desire. It will cause the prompt

ENTER THE DATE:

to be displayed on the screen. The computer will pause until you have entered the date and a RETURN. The date you enter will be stored in the memory variable DATE. Because this command occurs before the DO LOOP you will only need to enter the date one time for the entire set of rosters. Note that the command occurs before the printer is turned on.

PAGE HEADING

The page heading is printed by the use of the ? command. A ? used alone will cause a blank line to be printed and/or displayed. The text enclosed by apostrophes (delimiters) will be printed as shown in the example. (The delimiters don't get printed). Contents of memory variables or data fields will be printed when the variable name or the fieldname is used as shown.

```
? '        ',NAME,'        ',READING,'        ',MATH,'        ',RET
```

This produces the basic display format for each printed record. The blank spaces are used to position the column entries on the page. RET is a memory variable indicating whether or not the student was retained. The variable must be created and contain the proper information prior to this command line.

```
STORE ' ' TO RET
IF RETAINED
    STORE 'RETAINED' TO RET
ENDIF
```

These commands show one way to set up the memory variable RET for its later use. This process must be repeated for each data record.

As you can see, there is nothing difficult about preparing a procedure to prepare a special report. All that you need to do is be careful and methodical. Each step in the process must be entered into the computer. One very good approach is to add the SET PRINT ON command after you have the procedure working. This allows you to check out your procedure on the terminal without wasting paper.

SECTION FIVE

Now that we are expert programmers (and you thought programming was for computer people only!) Section Five illustrates how our database applications work in a practical business situation.

Our 'Video Store' example allows us to apply our database methods to the many procedures encountered when running a business. Our database management system accommodates a variety of services, from mailing lists and inventory needs to specialized transaction recording.

CHAPTER XV

BUSINESS USES

The whole idea of the microcomputer and database management is to help you. One very positive area in which they can help is the conduct of a small business. According to a recent report there are over three million businesses with gross revenues of less than $500,000 and that employ less than ten people.

A video store is a prime example of this type of small business. The Video Store specializes in the sale and rental of TV related items — primarily in Video Cassette Recorders (VCR's), Video Taped Movies, and related accessories. In addition to sale and rental of goods, these stores often sponsor 'video clubs' which entitles members to reduced rates on rentals and equipment.

There are several operations areas that can be appropriately supported by a database management system.

PAYROLL AND ACCOUNTING

STANDARD TAX REPORTING

INVENTORY MANAGEMENT

FLOORING CHARGES

MAILING LISTS

DAILY CASH REGISTER TALLEY

TRANSACTION RECORDING

This list is certainly not all-inclusive. However, it is fairly representative of areas easily supported by a DBMS. This support helps the owner manage his operation better and with less effort. We discuss the Video Store because it is particulary well suited to examples which explain the support concepts. There are very few specialized skills involved.

VIDEO STORE RENTAL

Renting out pre-recorded movies is a major part of the Video Store's business. The shop either purchases or leases movies for subsequent rental. Each tape represents an investment and takes up valuable shelf space. It is important to the owner to know which movies rent well and which don't. A movie which doesn't move should be disposed of, either by placing it 'on sale' or by returning it to the owner. It is also important to monitor how many times a popular movie is rented. Tapes do wear, and 'worn out' movies can result in unhappy (and probably, former) customers. A database management system can track such activities, for example reducing time required to monitor the number of times each tape is rented.

Many video stores operate a 'Video Club.' This scheme involves a fixed membership fee paid for providing significant discounts to members on movie rentals and other merchandise. These 'clubs' operate to the benefit of the store as well as the customer. A club member's list often forms the basis of a mailing list. A database management system can simplify mailing list maintenance and print out mailing labels, etc. It can also offer further support such as reminding the shop when a membership is due for renewal.

There are various other levels of record keeping which, without a computer, are done with pencil and paper. A computer system must perform additional services and/or reduce the amount of work involved to be a benefit.

Receipt of new merchandise requires the addition of the items to the inventory and accounts payable systems. Sale of an item requires a record of the sale as well as inventory system modifications. A database system easily accommodates inventory management as well as helping with most routine bookkeeping tasks such as accounts payable.

'Flooring' merchandise, similar to having goods on consignment, is a common business arrangement. The shop has the merchandise for a period of time (often about 90 days) before payment is due. Payment is due immediately if the merchandise is sold prior to the due date. Often a nominal 'flooring charge' is paid each month on unsold 'flooring'. Such 'flooring' arrangements require careful record keeping — a task easily supported with a database management system.

What good starting point might become the basis for a computer system? Since a pencil and paper database is familiar and useful to everyone, let's start there. We will exactly replace our old style database with a computer system database. Think first in terms of an overview of what work is involved.

On a typical business day several things might happen.

> New stock is received
> Stock is sold
> Club Memberships are sold
> Movies and equipment are rented
> Movies and equipment are returned
> Cash Register Transactions are Balanced

Each of these activities require paperwork. For example, a 'Cash Register Talley Sheet,' summarizing the day's business activity and accounting for all the money, must be completed each day. Such a form is shown as Figure 15-1.

CASH REGISTER TALLY SHEET

Day _____ Date _____

Person _____

COUNT MONEY FIRST AT OPENING

1. Beginning Total (Starting cash in drawer) $ _____

S A L E S

2. Rentals (Pre-recorded movies & equipment) $ _____

3. Memberships (Lifetime_____ Year _____ Other _____) $ _____

4. Services (Equipment repair & installation) $ _____

5. NON-TAXABLE Equipment & Accessories $ _____

6. Deposits (Prepayments) $ _____

7. TAXABLE Equipment & Accessories (Sales Tax included) $ _____

8. Total Sales (2+3+4+5+6+7) $ _____

9. Total Cash Paid Out (attach receipts) $ _____

10. Total Sales less Paid Out (8 minus 9) $ _____

COUNT MONEY IN REGISTER AT END OF DAY

11. Cash (15+16) $ _____

12. Checks (number of checks _____) $ _____

13. Charges (MasterCard and VISA) $ _____

14. Total Money in Register (11+12+13) $ _____

17. TOTAL (1+10) $ _____

18. Total Register (14) $ _____

Difference if any between #17 and #18 ☐ Short ☐ Extra $ _____

Z PRINT OUT AT END OF DAY $ _____

TOTAL CASH $ _____

Less starting cash for drawer $ _____

Amount for deposit $ _____

$ 1	
$ 2	
$ 5	
$ 10	
$ 20	
$ 50	
$100	

1¢	
5¢	
10¢	
25¢	
50¢	
$1	

15. TOTAL BILLS _____

16. TOTAL CHANGE _____

Figure 15-1

The activities summarized on this form constitute a large part of the store's day to day paperwork. The demonstration of appropriate database management support begins here. As with all our previous processes, Step #1 is PLANNING.

Planning must begin with a solid understanding of what is to be accomplished. So far we have identified several pieces of paper used in operating the store.

Duplicating each piece of paper with 'electronic paper' is an uncomplicated and useful way to get started. This allows you to build the system one piece at a time. You can easily check the results against the actual paperwork, thus providing a test computer system operation.

In our example, the clerk begins by selecting from a menu of possible 'electronic forms.' The beginning menu is shown in Screen 15-1.

```
SAMPLE VIDEO STORE MENU SYSTEM

        1 — MOVIE RENTAL

        2 — MEMBERSHIP

        3 — SALE

        4 — SERVICE

        5 — DEPOSITS

        6 — TALLEY SHEET

        7 — INVENTORY

        8 — QUIT

        Screen 15-1
```

A diagram of how these selections fit together is shown in Figure 15-2.

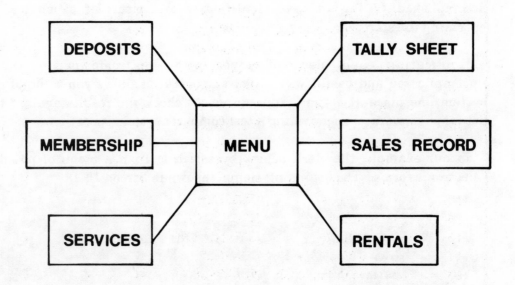

Figure 15-2

We first make the 'paper form' into an 'electronic form.' This requires a procedure and a database. The database plan — B:TALLEY — is shown in Figure 15-3.

FIELD	DESCRIPTION	FIELDNAME	TYPE	SIZE	DECIMALS
1.	Date	DATE	C	8	
2.	Name of Employee	NAME	C	10	
3.	Starting Cash	STARTCASH	N	6	2
4.	Total Rental Income	RENTALS	N	7	2
5.	Lifetime Memberships	LIFEMEMB	N	2	
6.	Yearly Memberships	YEARMEMB	N	2	
7.	Other Memberships	SPECMEMB	N	2	
8.	Membership Income	MEMBERSHIP	N	7	2
9.	Services Income	SERVICES	N	7	2
10.	Non Taxable Sales	NONTAXSALE	N	8	2
11.	Taxable Sales	TAXSALE	N	8	2
12.	Deposits	DEPOSITS	N	7	2
13.	Cash Paid Out (total)	PAIDOUT	N	7	2
14.	End of Day Cash	ENDCASH	N	8	2
15.	No. of Checks	NOCHECKS	N	3	
16.	Value of Checks	TOTALCHECK	N	8	2
17.	VISA and MasterCard	CHARGES	N	8	2
18.	Next day starting cash	NEXTCASH	N	6	2
19.	Amount for deposit	BANKED	N	8	2

Figure 15-3. Plan For Check Register Talley Sheet

One talley sheet equals one record in the talley sheet database. Several paper talley sheet items do not have corresponding fields in the electronic form because they result from calculations on items contained in the database.

Figure 15-4 shows a simple procedure allowing the clerk to fill out field entries. Lines beginning with NOTE are ignored by the computer. They are points of information for the operator describing how parts of the procedure work or what they are for.

In this particular procedure, the clerk manually enters all of the information for each day's operations, just as he would use the paper talley sheet. The computer, however, performs all the required calculations.

```
USE B:TALLEY
SET TALK OFF
GO BOTTOM
```
(After you set up database you must append at least one blank record or have some regular records in the database for this program to run)
```
IF .NOT.DATE=DATE( )
APPEND BLANK
REPLACE DATE WITH DATE( )
ENDIF
ERASE
@ 0,10 SAY 'CASH REGISTER TALLEY SHEET FOR' GET DATE
@ 2,10 SAY 'Name of Employee' GET NAME
@ 2,10 SAY 'Starting Cash' GET STARTCASH
@ 4,10 SAY 'Total Rental Income' GET RENTALS
@ 5,10 SAY 'Lifetime Memberships' GET LIFEMEMB
@ 6,10 SAY 'Yearly Memberships' GET YEARMEMB
@ 7,10 SAY 'Other Memberships' GET SPECMEMB
@ 8,10 SAY 'Membership Income' GET MEMBERSHIP
@ 9,10 SAY 'Services Income' GET SERVICES
@ 10,10 SAY 'Non Taxable Sales' GET NONTAXSALE
@ 11,10 SAY 'Taxable Sales' GET TAXSALE
@ 12,10 SAY 'Deposits' GET DEPOSITS
@ 13,10 SAY 'Cash Paid Out (total)' GET PAIDOUT
@ 14,10 SAY 'End of Day Cash' GET ENDCASH
@ 15,10 SAY 'Number of Checks' GET NOCHECKS
@ 16,10 SAY 'Value of Checks' GET TOTALCHECK
@ 17,10 SAY 'VISA and MasterCard Total' GET CHARGES
@ 18,10 SAY 'Next day starting cash' GET NEXTCASH
@ 19,10 SAY 'Amount for deposit' GET BANKED
READ
NOTE now we have all the data to compute cash register totals
```

(continued on next page)

```
STORE RENTALS+MEMBERSHIP+SERVICES+NONTAXSALE+TAXSALE
   +DEPOSITS TO TOTALSALES
STORE TOTALSALES-PAIDOUT+STARTCASH TO TOTAL
STORE ENDCASH+TOTALCHECK+CHARGES TO MONEY
ERASE
@  8,10 SAY  'STARTING CASH'  GET STARTCASH
@ 10,10 SAY  'TOTAL SALES'  GET TOTALSALES
@ 12,10 SAY  'AMOUNT OF CASH PAID OUT'  GET PAIDOUT
@ 14,10 SAY  'TOTAL MONEY IN REGISTER SHOULD BE'  GET TOTAL
@ 16,10 SAY  'TOTAL MONEY IN REGISTER IS'  GET MONEY
DO CASE
   CASE MONEY> TOTAL
   STORE MONEY—TOTAL TO DIFF
   @ 18,10 SAY  'REGISTER IS OVER BY'  GET DIFF
   CASE TOTAL> MONEY
   STORE TOTAL—MONEY TO DIFF
   @ 18,10 SAY  'REGISTER IS SHORT BY'  GET DIFF
ENDCASE
@ 20,5 SAY  'PRESS ANY KEY TO CONTINUE'
WAIT
SET TALK ON
RETURN
```

Figure 15-4

Potentially, the computer can do much more — for example help count cash and enter checks and charges similar to the check register examples in Chapter XI.

We spoke briefly before of typical 'Video Club' memberships in this type of business. When such a membership is sold, the clerk fills out a form containing:

1. Member's Name
2. Member's Address
3. Member's Phone Number
4. Video Club Membership Number
5. Membership Fee
6. Kind of Membership (life,yearly,etc.)
7. Date of Membership

This form becomes a single record in your membership database file, called B:MEMBERS in this example. B:MEMBERS database plan is shown in Figure 15-5.

FIELD	DESCRIPTION	FIELDNAME	TYPE	SIZE	DECIMALS
1.	Date	DATE	C	8	
2.	Name of Member	MEMBNAME	C	30	
3.	Street Address	ADDRESS	C	20	
4.	City	CITY	C	20	
5.	Zip Code	ZIP	C	5	
6.	Telephone Number	PHONE	C	8	
7.	Kind of Membership	KINDMEMB	C	1	
8.	Membership Fee	FEE	N	6	2
9.	Membership Number	MEMBERNO	C	8	

Figure 15-5. Plan For Video Club Membership

The database procedure allowing new member 'registration' is extremely simple. Named B:MEMBERS, it is shown in Figure 15-6.

```
USE B:MEMBERS
SET TALK OFF
ERASE
GO BOTTOM
STORE VAL(MEMBERNO)+1 TO M1
APPEND BLANK
REPLACE MEMBERNO WITH STR(M1,8),DATE WITH DATE()
@  3,10 SAY 'SAMPLE COMPUTER MEMBERSHIP FORM'
@  8,10 SAY 'MEMBERSHIP NUMBER'  GET MEMBERNO
@  8,40 SAY 'DATE'  GET DATE
CLEAR GETS
@ 10,10 SAY 'Name of Member'  GET MEMBNAME
@ 12,10 SAY 'Street Address'  GET ADDRESS
@ 14,10 SAY 'City'  GET CITY
@ 16,10 SAY 'Zip Code'  GET ZIP
@ 18,10 SAY 'Telephone Number'  GET PHONE
@ 20,10 SAY 'Kind of Membership (L — life Y — Year R — Renewel)'  GET KIND
READ
DO CASE
  CASE KINDMEMB='L'
    REPLACE FEE WITH 100.00
  CASE KINDMEMB='Y'
    REPLACE FEE WITH 50.00
  CASE KINDMEMB='R'
    REPLACE FEE WITH 25.00
ENDCASE
CLEAR GETS
@ 22,10 SAY 'Membership Fee'  GET FEE
READ
SET TALK ON
RETURN
```

Figure 15-6

In establishing this procedure, we arrive at an important point. We can link the membership form (once we are sure it works correctly) back to the 'Cash Register Talley Sheet.' Such linkage is particularly easy in this example as memberships were added manually and talley sheet data was entered manually. Now a membership sale can automatically update the talley sheet.

Business Uses

This is accomplished by a simple addition to the procedure B:MEMBERS shown in Figure 15-6. The addition inserted between READ and SET TALK ON is shown in Figure 15-7.

```
READ (THIS IS THE READ SHOWN IN FIGURE 15-6)
STORE KINDMEMB TO A1
STORE FEE TO A2
USE B:TALLEY
GO BOTTOM
IF .NOT.DATE=DATE( )
   APPEND BLANK
   REPLACE DATE WITH DATE( )
ENDIF
DO CASE
   CASE A1='L'
      REPLACE LIFEMEMB WITH LIFEMEMB+1
      REPLACE MEMBERSHIP WITH MEMBERSHIP+A2
   CASE A1='Y'
      REPLACE YEARMEMB WITH YEARMEMB+1
      REPLACE MEMBERSHIP WITH MEMBERSHIP+A2
   CASE A1='R'
      REPLACE SPECMEMB WITH SPECMEMB+1
      REPLACE MEMBERSHIP WITH MEMBERSHIP+A2
ENDCASE
SET TALK ON (THIS IS ALSO FROM FIGURE 14-6)
```

Figure 15-7

In this membership example we add all information to the membership database B:MEMBERS. At the same time, without any effort, we are able to update the Cash Register Talley Sheet.

A major part of this business is renting of video taped movies. These movies may be either owned or leased by the store. When a movie is rented to a customer a form is filled out and signed by the customer. The form contains

1. Customer's Name
2. Customer's Address
3. Customer's Phone Number
4. Driver's License Number
        or
   Video Club Membership Number
5. Rental Fee
6. Amount of Deposit (if any)
        (club members avoid deposits)
7. Number of Movies Rented
8. Names of Movies Rented
9. Date rented
10. Date to be returned

When the movies are returned, the form is 'canceled.' The store uses this form to help keep track of:

The cash transaction
Where the movies are
How many times each movie has been rented

At first glance, the straightforward way to handle the rental business on your computer would be to have one record for each transaction. The only problem with this approach is item 8. How do you decide about the amount of space required for a field to handle the names of the movies. If we do this with a paper form we can write small. You can't write small with a computer.

The way to handle this problem is to use more than one file for the rental database. The first file will contain all of the required information except for the movie titles. The title of each movie rented will become a record in the second database. The two databases will be linked together with a transaction identifier. This transaction identifier must be unique for the transaction. It can require one or more fields. In this example, the unique transaction identification can be provided by the customer's Drivers License number (or membership number) and the date.

Business Uses

The tie between the two database files is shown more graphically in Figure 15-8. The information that is to be contained in these two files is shown in two side-by-side columns.

RENTAL DATABASE	MOVIE TITLE DATABASE
1. Customer's Name	
2. Customer's Address	
3. Customer's Phone Number	
4. Rental Fee	
5. Amount of Deposit (if any) (club members avoid deposits)	
6. Number of Movies Rented	
7. Number of Days Rented	
8. Club Member (y/n)	
9. Driver's License Number or Video Club Membership Number	Driver's License Number or Video Club Membership Number
10. Data Rented	Date Rented
11.	Movie Title
12.	VHS or BETA

Figure 15-8

At this point we believe that the combination of the date and the driver's license number is unique enough to identify each transaction. Each rental transaction results in a 'Rental Database' record. There will be one 'Movie Title Database' record for each movie rented. This means that if a customer rents four movies the 'Movie Title Database' will have four movies added to it. Those titles are 'related' to the rental record by the license number and the date.

We now have the core of the idea. However, this example will require a lot of typing on the part of the clerk. All of the customer information as well as the movie titles must be filled in. Fortunately, in many cases, we can minimize the typing by making use of information already stored in the computer.

256

Many of the rental customers will be members of the store's Video Club. The membership database can also be linked to the rental database (when a member is involved) by the membership number. The membership information can be copied to the rental database — saving the clerk both time and effort (as well as minimizing the chance for error). This is also a terrific opportunity to add non-members to this database — thereby increasing its use as a Mailing List. When a field is used as a tie to link two database files together the field should be the same size and type in both database files. 'Alpha ' is not the same as 'Alpha' to the computer. It considers the blank spaces also.

Movie titles are (or should be) a field in the Movie Rental Inventory Database. Basic inventory information includes:

    Movie Title
    VHS or BETA
    Shelf Location
    Date Purchased or Leased by Store
    Purchase Price/Lease Rate
    Owned or Leased
    Supplier

The movie title is an awkward way for the store to deal with movie records. An identification number would enable the clerk to work more quickly and accurately with or without the computer. In our example we will assume that a five digit identification number has been assigned to each rental movie.

If we add a few fields to the inventory database we can use it in place of the 'Movie Title Database.'

    Rental Fee
    Drivers License or Membership Number
    Rental Date
    Number of Times Rented
    Rented (Y/N)

There are a number of possible file combinations that one could use for this example. Each has advantages and disadvantages depending upon the specific application. For the purposes of our example we will use the Inventory Database in the place of the Movie Title Database from now on.

A diagram of this rental procedure (so far) looks like that shown in Figure 15-9.

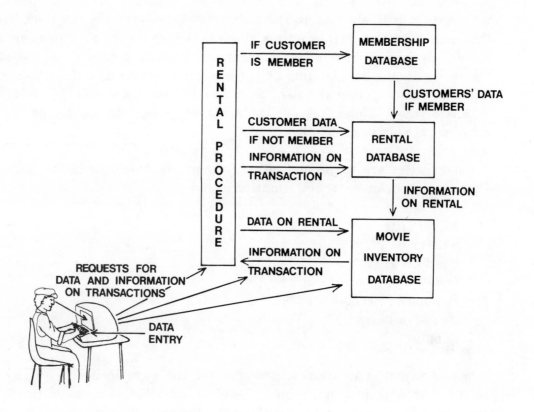

Figure 15-9

Let's take a look at where we are. When a customer rents a movie, the clerk fills out a 'computer form.' This form becomes a single record in a rental database. The rental inventory database is used to identify the movies rented out. The drivers license number or club membership number and the rental date are common fields in the two database files. These two fields serve to tie the two files together. Each time a movie is rented the 'number of times rented' field gets increased by one. If the customer is a club member much of the information is automatically retrieved from the membership database.

Taking the inevitable next step finds the computer calculating the total rental fee and adding this to the receipt. Just as in the last example, the value of the transaction can be automatically added to the Talley Sheet.

Now let's put all of this together. A diagram of this database system is shown in Figure 15-10.

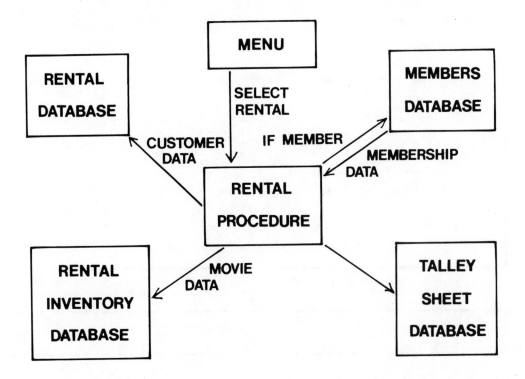

Figure 15-10

The process outlined above is a reasonable example of one way in which a computer system can be used to help with the operation of a small business. It is not the only way, and it is not necessarily the best way. However, it provides a useful demonstration of an approach to solving a business problem with a computer.

The next step is to write down the database plans for each of the database files used in this process. The plan for the membership file was already described in Figure 15-5. The two 'new' database files are shown in Figures 15-11, and 15-12. A procedure that will perform the rental process described above is shown in Figure 15-13. One word of caution. This procedure is intended to illustrate the process. It is necessarily somewhat simplified from one that you might use for an actual business.

FIELD	DESCRIPTION	FIELDNAME	TYPE	SIZE	DECIMALS
1.	Customer's Name	CNAME	C	30	
2.	Street Address	CADDRESS	C	20	
3.	City	CCITY	C	20	
4.	Zip Code	CZIP	C	5	
5.	Telephone Number	CPHONE	C	8	
6.	Identification	ID	C	8	
7.	Rental Fee	RFEE	N	5	2
8.	Amount of Deposit	CDEPOSIT	N	6	2
9.	Number of Rentals	CRENTAL	N	2	
10.	Number of Days Rented	CTIME	N	2	
11.	Club Member (Y/N)	CMEMBER	L	1	
12.	Date Rented	CDATE	C	8	

Figure 15-11. Rental Database Plan

FIELD	DESCRIPTION	FIELDNAME	TYPE	SIZE	DECIMALS
1.	Movie Title	TITLE	C	30	
2.	VHS or BETA	VHS	L	1	
3.	Location	LOCATION	C	5	
4.	Date Acquired	IDATE	C	8	
5.	Price/Lease Rate	COST	C	5	2
6.	Owned or Leased	OWNED	L	1	
7.	Supplier	SUPPLIER	C	20	
8.	Identification	RID	C	8	
9.	Rental Charge	RCHARGE	N	4	2
10.	Rental Date	RDATE	C	8	
11.	No. of Times Rented	RCOUNT	N	3	
12.	Rented (Y/N)	RENTED	L	1	
13.	Movie ID Number	MOVIEID	C	5	

Figure 15-12. Inventory Database

The procedure described in Figure 15-13 is the most elaborate in this book. While elaborate, it is not difficult. Most of the instructions are for screen displays.

This procedure introduces one new command — SELECT. This dBASE II command allows the computer to work with two database files at the same time. So far we have worked with only one database at a time. Each time that we selected a database file with the USE command the database system was positioned to the first record in the file. In this example we will be going from the database B:RENTAL to other database files and back to B:RENTAL. SELECT will allow us to 'keep our place' in the file B:RENTAL.

When using two database files simultaneously, one is termed the PRIMARY file, the other the SECONDARY. You can switch back and forth between the two files without losing your place in either.

```
USE B:RENTAL
SET TALK OFF
APPEND BLANK
REPLACE CDATE WITH DATE( )
ERASE
@ 1,15 SAY 'SAMPLE VIDEO RENTAL FORM'
@ 2,15 SAY 'IS THE CUSTOMER A CLUB MEMBER (Y/N)' GET CMEMBER
READ
CLEAR GETS                (keeps the computer from asking the question again)
IF CMEMBER
   @ 8,10 SAY 'ENTER THE MEMBERSHIP NUMBER' GET ID
   READ
   SELECT SECONDARY        (tells the computer there will be two files)
   USE B:MEMBERS           (names the second file)
   LOCATE FOR MEMBERNO=ID
   SELECT PRIMARY          (returns to first database at desired record)
   The following is a transfer of data from the located record in B:MEMBERS to
   the new record in B:RENTAL
   REPLACE CNAME WITH MEMBNAME,CADDRESS WITH ADDRESS,CCITY WITH
CITY,CZIP WITH ZIP,CPHONE WITH PHONE
ENDIF
```

(continued on next page)

```
        @ 3,10 SAY 'CUSTOMERS NAME' GET CNAME
        @ 4,10 SAY 'CUSTOMERS ADDRESS' GET CADDRESS
        @ 5,10 SAY '          CITY' GET CCITY
        @ 6,10 SAY 'ZIP CODE' GET CZIP
        @ 7,10 SAY 'TELEPHONE NUMBER' GET CPHONE
IF CMEMBER
   CLEAR GETS
ELSE
        @ 8,10 SAY 'DRIVERS LICENSE NUMBER' GET ID
        @ 9,10 SAY 'ENTER AMOUNT OF DEPOSIT' GET CDEPOSIT
ENDIF
        @ 10,10 SAY 'NUMBER OF DAYS RENTED' GET CTIME
        @ 10,40 SAY 'NUMBER OF MOVIES RENTED' GET CRENTAL
        READ
        CLEAR GETS
        SELECT SECONDARY          (select secondary or choose new secondary file)
        USE B:INVENTRY
        STORE CRENTAL TO X
        DO WHILE X>0
           STORE '      ' TO MOVIENO
           @ 12,10 SAY 'MOVIE IDENTIFICATION NUMBER' GET MOVIENO
           READ
           LOCATE FOR MOVIEID=MOVIENO
           REPLACE RDATE WITH DATE( ),RCOUNT WITH RCOUNT+1,RENTED WITH Y
           REPLACE RID WITH ID
           SELECT PRIMARY
           REPLACE RFEE WITH RFEE+RCHARGE
           STORE X-1 TO X
ENDDO
SELECT SECONDARY
USE B:TALLEY
GO BOTTOM
IF .NOT.DATE=DATE( )
   APPEND BLANK
   REPLACE DATE WITH DATE( )
ENDIF
REPLACE DEPOSITS WITH CDEPOSIT+DEPOSITS
REPLACE RENTALS WITH RENTALS+RFEE
SELECT PRIMARY                    (back to B:RENTALS)
ERASE
```

```
@ 5,10 SAY 'CUSTOMER'S NAME' GET CNAME
@ 7,10 SAY 'MOVIE RENTAL CHARGE' GET RFEE
IF CDEPOSIT> 0
@ 7,40 SAY 'REQUIRED DEPOSIT' GET CDEPOSIT
ENDIF
STORE CDEPOSIT+RFEE TO DUE
@ 9,10 SAY 'TOTAL AMOUNT DUE' GET DUE
CLEAR GETS
SELECT SECONDARY
USE B:INVENTRY
DISPLAY OFF TITLE,RCHARGE FOR RID=ID.AND.RDATE=DATE( )
SELECT PRIMARY
SET TALK ON
RETURN
```

Figure 15-13

In this example, the computer first checks to see if the customer is a club member. If so, it asks for the club membership number, uses the membership file, and enters the relevent data such as name, address, etc. into the rental file. If not, it prompts the clerk to enter each of the these data items. Once this is completed it will prompt the clerk to enter the information regarding the business transaction. Following this it will select the inventory file and enter the required data items

Rental Date (RDATE)
Customers Identification (drivers license or membership number)

for each movie rented. In addition, it will change the number of times rented field and indicate that the movie is now rented. It then returns to the rental database and adds the movie rental charge to the contents of the fee field (RFEE). Once this has been completed the 'Cash Register Talley Sheet' is automatically updated with the rental fee and the deposit information.

In the final step the computer displays basic elements of the transaction including the customer's name, the amount due, and the names of the movies rented.

Business Uses

This example is particulary significant. There are four separate database files used. The procedure isolates you (and the clerk) from all of the database activity. As the information is filled in the database management system moves from database to database adding and changing information as necessary.

The procedure B:RENTAL covers the basic elements in managing the movie rental aspects of this business. You should NOT consider that it would be adequate to operate the movie rental business. The procedure has not considered all possible details that should be covered in a business procedure. Some elements were omitted in order to better illustrate the concepts of working with video screen 'forms' and multiple database files.

A FEW CLOSING REMARKS

Throughout this book we have demonstrated database management as an easy, effective and natural way for you to get results from your computer. In illustrating various database concepts we have used everyday examples to demonstrate the simple and versatile features of a database management system.

In retrospect, we realize that 'database' is a concept we have long been familiar with. The specific terminology used in computer database systems may be a little unfamiliar, but it certainly isn't difficult. It doesn't take long to begin thinking of a column of data as a field. Nor does it take much effort to think of the title of the database as a filename. Once you have mastered the simple terminology it is easy to master the system so that it works for you.

This, of course, is the whole idea behind microcomputer database management systems. They are supposed to do the work while you do the thinking. There is no need to become a computer specialist to make the computer work for you — you have seen in this book how really simple it is to make the computer work. Whether business or home oriented, a database management system provides the first time user with an excellent opportunity to both increase his work efficiency and acquaint himself with computers. For the specialist, there is also increased efficiency as well continuing satisfaction in the effective use of computing tools.

While you are still learning about your database management system, work with the applications that provide the most return for your effort. Remember our Liquor Store Inventory — we actually did much less work when using the computer than if we had performed the inventory without it. By starting with simple applications you will find it easy to progress to the more complex ones — after all, you didn't run a marathon the first time you went to the track.

A common error is to purchase a computer and a database management system because you have a complicated problem to solve — and then as your first task, jump in and try to solve that complicated problem. If this happens, you make your problem (and your life) unnecessarily complex. You really need to become familiar with the computer and your software first. It is too much to expect to establish the relationship of your problem (especially if it is complicated) to the hardware and software all at the same time.

To familiarize yourself with your system we suggest you practice — construct 'learning' problems that use small databases. The examples provided in this book should help direct you in constructing examples of your own. THE SOLUTIONS TO COMPLICATED PROBLEMS ARE MADE UP OF MANY SIMPLE PIECES. It is much to your advantage to construct 'learning' problems using small databases because they allow you to easily check your results to see whether or not you are getting the 'right answer.' This is great background for dealing with larger and larger databases. The examples in this book are varied enough to give you a good idea of an approach to a specific problem if you select the appropriate pieces from one or more examples and then assemble them into your solution. While it is valuable to work through the examples, you will learn more quickly by using them as a guide to work out a solution for a problem of your own.

Once you select the 'learning' problem you'd like to construct, study your problem carefully and plan your solution methodically. If you understand your problems and are methodical in your planning and the subsequent implementation of your system, you will always be successful. These three ingredients — understanding the problem, planning and methodical (step by step) implementation — are essential to success in any computer system.

Success in the solution of an initial 'easy' problem will give you the experience and confidence to begin attacking more and more complex problems. And as you do so, you will discover that these complex problems aren't difficult after all. Take a step by step approach, become familiar with the language, and you will have a winner.

We hope this book will be a useful guide to you as you learn to master a useful and versatile tool — the computer. Database management is probably the surest and most direct course towards attaining that goal. With it, we are sure you will find the computer a most helpful servant.

266

GLOSSARY

.AND.

A Boolean operator that is used to join two logic expressions so that the resulting expression applies to the shared characteristics of the expression. For example: GRADE = '3'.AND.ROOM = '122' restricts the expression to third graders who are assigned to room 122.

.NOT.

A Boolean operator which is used to invoke the opposite of the expression. For example: .NOT.GRADE = '3' means all grades except the third.

.OR.

A Boolean operator which is used to join two groups within a logic expression. For example, the third and fourth grades can be joined within the logical expression GRADE = '3'.OR.GRADE = '4'.

?

A dBASE II command for displaying selected items.

@

A dBASE operator that is used in conjuction with the SAY and GET commands to generate displays on either the CRT or the printer.

*

Normally used to indicate multiplication in computer systems. In dBASE II it is also used to indicate database records that have been marked for deletion.

#

The 'pound sign' is used as a multipurpose function. It is normally used as a shorthand for 'not equal to.' In dBASE II it is also used as a symbol for 'record number.' For example: DISPLAY FOR # = 3 would display the third data record.

!

A symbol which, in dBASE II, tells the computer to not distinguish between upper and lower case characters.

$

A dBASE II operator that allows you to search for a sequence of characters contained in a field or a memory variable. It is often called either a substring or string operator. It can be interpreted as meaning 'contained in.' For example: 'Robert' $NAME would allow you to search the field NAME for the character string ROBERT.

ACCEPT TO [memory variable name]

A dBASE II command which allows the input of character strings into designated memory variables without need for delimiters. Normally used within procedures (dBASE II command files).

ADL

Applications Development Language — the computer language used with dBASE II.

APPEND

The dBASE II command to add records to a database.

APPEND BLANK

A variation of APPEND which adds blank records to a database. Normally used within procedures.

APPEND FROM < filename>

Used to append data from the named file to the file in use.

BACKUP

The process of copying a disk or diskfile to another disk for protection against possible future failure. Also the backup copy of the file or disk.

BASIC

A computer language. An acronym standing for Beginners All Purpose Symbolic Instruction Code.

BOOLEAN

A method of computer logic based on the work of George Boole, who developed a certain type of Algebra.

BOOTING

The process of starting up the computer.

BROWSE

A dBASE II command used for editing. Several records are displayed simultaneously for full screen editing.

BYTE

The amount of memory required to store a character such as an 'A' or '#' or '9.'

CANCEL

A command used to terminate a procedure and return control of the computer to the keyboard.

CASE

A variation of the IF statement. Case can only be used within DO CASE/ENDCASE.

CHANGE

A dBASE II command used for editing.

CHARACTER

Any keyboard symbol that can be printed such as an 'A' or '$' or '1' or 'a' (includes blank spaces).

CHARACTER FIELD

A database field that is intended to contain characters.

CHARACTER STRING

A continuous sequence of characters such as 'John Doe.'

CHR( )

A dBASE II command which allows you direct control of the peripheral devices such as the printer and the CRT.

CLEAR

This command resets dBASE II. All databases in USE are closed, all memory variables are released, and the system is just as it would be when you initially enter dBASE II.

CLEAR GETS

A command which removes all pending GETS internally without altering the screen (as the ERASE command would). This will limit the domain of a READ to only those GETS issued after the CLEAR GETS command.

COBOL

A computer language used extensively in mainframe business application. The first English like computer language. An acronym for Committee On Business Oriented Languages.

COMMAND

dBASE II terminology for a computer instruction.

COMMAND FILE

A set of computer instructions stored or saved on a disk for repetitive use. dBASE II terminology for a computer procedure.

CONDITION

A logical expression that can be used to more explicitly define a command such as DISPLAY. DISPLAY FOR NAME = 'JOHN DOE' modifies the command DISPLAY so that it applies only for records meeting the condition NAME = 'JOHN DOE'.

CONDITIONAL REPLACEMENT

A technique for changing the contents of a database where the replace command is modified by a condition. REPLACE TEACHER WITH 'ADAMS' FOR ROOM = '171' will replace the contents of the field TEACHER with 'ADAMS' for only those records meeting the condition ROOM = '171'.

CONTINUE

A command which positions to next record with conditions specified in the LOCATE command.

CONTROL KEY

A key which potentially gives a third value to all of the keys of the keyboard. Similar to the shift key which gives a second meaning to each of the keys of the keyboard.

COPY TO <filename>

A dBASE II command which copies the database in use to the named database. Used to create a copy of the database for backup. Variations exist which will allow you to copy only selected parts of the database in use to the named database.

COUNT

A data displaying command which counts the number of records that meet some conditional expression.

CP/M®

Control Program/Microcomputer. A popular operating system for microcomputers. CP/M® is a registered trademark of Digital Research Corporation.

CPU

Central Processing Unit — the central processor of the computer system. It contains the main storage, arithmetic unit and special register groups.

CREATE

The dBASE II command to allow you to establish the structure of a new database file.

CRT

Cathode Ray Tube. Popularly used to denote the video display device used in conjunction with computers.

CTRL KEY

Control Key — used in combination with various keys to give them a second meaning and function.

DASD

Direct Access Storage Device such as a disk.

DATA

A piece of information. Normally useless as an independent item. Can convey information when used with another item of data. For example, the phone number 555-3213 is relatively useless by itself. It conveys information when used in conjunction with another data item, Butch Johnson.

DATABASE

A repository of stored information organized in such a way that data is easily retrieved. Normally associated with an organized base of data stored within a computer that is useable by multiple applications. An everyday example of a non-computer database is the telephone directory.

DBMS

Database Management System.

DEFAULT

When the computer receives a command it must take some action. Unless otherwise instructed it will take a preprogrammed action. That pre-programmed action is called the default.

DELETE

A dBASE II command which marks records for deletion (see also PACK).

DELIMITERS

A way of identifying character strings to the computer. For example it allows the computer to distinguish between the field NAME and the word 'NAME'.

DISK DRIVE

A mechanical device used to read and write information onto a disk.

DISKS

A circular plate, coated with magnetic material, for storing data. The medium on which a computer may permanently or temporarily store information to be used or read at a later date.

DISPLAY

A dBASE II command to display the contents of a data record.

DISPLAY ALL

A variation of the DISPLAY command. This variation will display all records of the database in use — pausing every 15 records.

DISPLAY FILES ON < drive id>

A dBASE II command which displays the filename, number of records, and date of last change of all database files on the named disk.

DISPLAY FOR < condition >
> A variation of the DISPLAY command. The FOR < condition > clause modifies the DISPLAY command so that all records meeting the condition will be displayed 15 at a time.

DISPLAY MEMORY
> A variation of the DISPLAY command which will display the name, type, size, and content of all memory variables.

DISPLAY OFF
> A variation of DISPLAY which displays the database record without the record number.

DISPLAY STRUCTURE
> A variation of the DISPLAY command which is used to display the structure of the database currently in use.

DO < filename >
> A dBASE II command which instructs the computer to execute the named procedure (command file).

DO CASE
> A dBASE II command which is used as an alternative to multiple nested IF, ENDIF statements. It must be accompanied by an ENDCASE command. Normally used in procedures.

DO WHILE < condition >
> A dBASE II command which tells the computer to repeatedly execute the sequence of commands between the DO WHILE statement and its concluding ENDDO statement as long as the condition is satisfied. Used in dBASE II command files (procedures).

DOS
> Disk Operating System — software.

EDIT < record number >
> A command which allows changing of a data field contents. In dBASE II it invokes a full screen operation which allows you to change the contents of desired fields by moving the cursor to the appropriate location and typing in the new data.

EJECT

A dBASE II command which ejects a page on the printer.

ELSE

A command file alternate path of command execution within IF.

ENDCASE

A command file command that terminates DO CASE.

ENDDO

A command file terminator for DO WHILE command.

ENDIF

A command file terminator for IF command.

EOF

End Of File — a dBASE II function; also a special ASCII file character.

ERASE

A command which clears the CRT.

ESCAPE

A key used on many computers which allows you to interrupt a procedure or a command execution from the keyboard. And on many computers that have no ESCAPE key, a CTRL [is used.

FIELD

In systems such as dBASE II, a field contains an item of information. It corresponds to a column of information on a paper database.

FIELD DESCRIPTION

A field description consists of three parts: the field name, field type, and the field width including decimal places (if any).

FIELDNAME

The field 'title.' Containing ten or fewer characters, must begin with a letter, and may not contain blank spaces.

FIELD SIZE

The number of character positions needed to contain the data to be placed in the field.

FIELDTYPE

The kind of data that may be stored in a field. The three fieldtypes are character, numeric, and logical.

FIELDWIDTH

The number of spaces needed in the field to contain the data.

FILE

A collection of information such as database file or a command file stored as an identifiable unit on a disk.

FILENAME

Used to identify the file to the computer. Must contain eight or fewer characters, must begin with a letter, and may not contain any blank spaces.

FILETYPE

A three character extension on the filename following the filename and a period. Used to distinguish among different file types with the same name and to identify to the computer certain kinds of files which it has been programmed to deal with in a specific way. As an example, .DBF file is recognized by dBASE II as a database file.

FIND < key >

A dBASE II command to find the record with the key. May be used only with indexed files.

FLOPPIES

Floppy disks.

FLOPPY DISK

A storage medium commonly used on microcomputers. Information is stored on a thin flexible mylar disk.

FLOPPY DISK SYSTEM

A computer system which uses floppy disks.

FORTRAN

A traditional computer language used mainly in scientific application. Acronym for Formula Translation.

GET

A dBASE II command which is used in conjunction with the @ command to display the contents of a field or a memory variable. When used in conjunction with the READ command, the contents of the field of memory variable may be changed by simply typing in the new information.

GO BOTTOM

A command which makes dBASE II go to the last record in the database being used.

GO TOP

A command which makes dBASE II go to the first record in the database being used.

GOTO < record number>

This command is used to reposition the record pointer of the database to the named record number.

HARD DISK

A disk which is a rigid metal plate covered with magnetic film; capable of storing large amounts of data.

HARD DISK SYSTEM

A computer system which uses hard disks.

I/O

A mechanism by which the computer accepts and distributes the information among the peripheral devices. An acronym for Input/Output.

IF < condition>

A statement that tells the computer to execute a set of commands provided that a condition is satisfied.

INDEX ON < fieldlist> TO < filename>

A dBASE II command which creates an index file with the named filename. The index file causes the contents of the database file to appear to be arranged in the logical order of the contents of the listed fields.

INPUT TO < memory variable name >

A dBASE II command which allows keyboard input of numeric data to a memory variable. Only numeric data will be accepted. Normally used within procedures.

INSERT

A dBASE II command which inserts a new data record into the middle of a database file.

INT ( )

A function which will round off a number which has a decimal by throwing away everything to the right of the decimal point. Short for integer.

JOIN

A command which outputs the JOIN of two relational databases.

KEYBOARD

A device similar to a typewriter keyboard by which a user may "talk" to a computer.

LEN (memory variable name)

A dBASE II function that tells you how many characters are in the named string memory variable.

LIST

A dBASE II command to display all data records in a database continuously.

LOCATE FOR < condition >

A dBASE II command used to find a record that satisfies the condition.

LOGICAL FIELDS

Fields with only two possible contents. Used when there will only be two possible mutually exclusive entries such as 'T' and 'F' or 'Y' and 'N' or 'M' and 'F'.

LOGICAL RECORDS

Records in an index file or another similar file which are 'images' of part of the actual data. Normally used as an aid to using the actual data.

LOOP

A command which causes execution of a command file to skip back to the beginning of DO WHILE. It is used as an escape when some undesired condition is encountered.

MASS MEMORY

Peripheral storage devices such as disk drives and tape drives.

MEMORY VARIABLE

Allows you to store information in the computers main memory for your temporary use. Similar in concept to memory on an electronic calculator. All information is lost when machine is turned off.

MENU

A computer procedure that displays a set of choices for action.

MENU SYSTEM

A computer procedure that uses a menu selection to choose a course of action for the computer to follow.

MICROCOMPUTER

A small computer designed principally for use by a single person.

MILLISECOND

1/1000th of a second.

MINICOMPUTER

A small computer that is generally configured for simultaneous use by a small number of people. Slightly larger and more powerful than a microcomputer.

MODIFY STRUCTURE

A dBASE II command that allows you to change the structure of a database. Changing the structure will usually destroy the database contents. The command should be used with care.

MODIFY COMMAND

A dBASE II command that allows you to create and/or edit the contents of a procedure (command file).

NOTE <text material>

A dBASE II command (normally used in procedures) which causes the computer to ignore the text that is written on the line. Used to describe the procedure for future reference.

NUMERIC FIELDS

Fields that contain numbers that are meant to be used in numeric calculation.

OPERATING SYSTEM

Software that makes your computer hardware system into a computer.

PACK

A command which physically DELETEs all records marked for deletion.

PASCAL

A computer language having some of the features of dBASE II.

PERIPHERALS

Devices used with the computer such as a printer and disk drives.

PHYSICAL RECORDS

The actual data records.

PIP

A CP/M® command that allows you to copy computer files from one disk to another.

PL/1

A computer language.

POINTER

A software mechanism that directs the computer to the database record of interest.

PRIMARY KEY

A unique way of identifying the record that is directly usable by the computer system. In dBASE II, the PRIMARY KEY is the record number.

PRINTER

A peripheral device which outputs data from the computer onto paper.

PROGRAM

A series of commands to be executed by the computer as a unit. A procedure is a program. In dBASE II a command file is a program.

PROGRAMMER

Any person who writes programs.

PROMPT

An indication from the computer that it is ready to accept keyboard commands. Also a request for specific information to be input from the keyboard.

QUERY

A user request for information from the computer. Normally a keyboard request.

QUIT

A command that causes dBASE II to close all files currently being used and exit to the operating system.

RAM

An acronym for Random Access Memory. This is normally the computer's main memory. Random access memory is really computer memory that is directly addressable and can be written to as well as read from.

READ

A dBASE II command which is used in conjunction with the GET command to perform full screen (cursor) editing of the contents of memory variables and data fields.

RECALL

A dBASE II command which "undeletes" records previously marked for deletion.

RECORD

An integral unit of data items. In dBASE II, it is that information which is contained on a row in a rectangular table of rows and columns.

RECORD LOCKOUT

An artifice to protect against possible simultaneous editing of a single data item in systems where there may be more than one user at a time.

RECORD NUMBER

An identifying number assigned to each data record by the database management system. The record number is unique for each record (no two records have the same record number).

RELATIONAL DATABASE SYSTEM

A type of database management system based on the use of rectangular tables of rows and columns. Different database files are linked (related) by the contents of a data field where the field contents may be common to both database files.

RELEASE < memory variable names>

A dBASE II command which 'erases' the named memory variables.

RENAME < filename 1> TO < filename 2>

A dBASE II command to rename a file. The file cannot be currently in use.

REPLACE < fieldname> WITH < new contents>

A dBASE command which replaces the contents of the named data field with the desired new contents. Most often used within procedures. May be effectively used from the keyboard in conjunction with FOR < condition>.

REPORT

A dBASE II command which prepares a report based on the contents of a database and your answers to a series of simple questions. The report is displayed on the CRT. The answers to the questions are entered from the keyboard for the first use of a specific report. The answers are saved in a .FRM file and the report will thereafter be generated automatically. There may be many reports available at any one time.

REPORT TO PRINT

A variation of REPORT that causes the report to be printed.

RETURN

A command which ends a command file and returns to the next higher procedure. Control returns to the keyboard if there is no higher procedure.

RETURN KEY

Similar to the carriage return key on a typewriter. Should probably be labeled as ENTER on a computer terminal.

ROM

An acronym for Read Only Memory.

RUB

A key which deletes the character to the left of the cursor.

SAVE

A command which copies the currently defined memory variables to mass storage.

SAY

A dBASE II command used in conjunction with the @ operator to display the information on the CRT or the printer.

SELECT PRIMARY

A command that selects the PRIMARY database.

SELECT SECONDARY

A command that selects the SECONDARY database.

SEQUENTIAL ACCESS

An access method for data records whereby the computer examines each record sequentially — beginning with the first record — until the desired record(s) are located.

SET ECHO ON/OFF

All commands which come from a command file are echoed on the screen as if they had been entered from the keyboard. ECHO is normally off and must be turned on if needed.

SET PRINT ON/OFF

Routes the computer output to the printer. Normally output is not directed to the printer.

SET TALK ON/OFF

The results from commands are normally displayed on the CRT. This is often undesirable when using command files.

SKIP [n]

A command which positions the database forwards or backwards a number of records.

SORT

A command which will cause the database to be physically rearranged into some desired order — normally by the numerical value of some fields(s) or alphabetically according to the contents of a character field.

STORE

A command which stores data into memory variables.

STRUCTURE

The predefined organization of your database. It is established by the fieldname, fieldtype, and fieldwidth.

SUM < fieldname>

A command that adds the contents of the named fields.

TERMINAL

The means with which you communicate with your computer and it communicates with you. The most popular terminal devices with microcomputers are video display terminals.

TYPE

This function is the data type function and yields a 'C', 'N', or 'L' depending on whether the one-character string is, respectively, Character, Numeric, Logical or 'U' undefined.

UPDATE

A command which merges records from two databases.

USE < filename>

A command which tells dBASE II which database you want to work with.

VAL(x)

Allows the contents of a character data field or memory variable to be used in arithmetic calculations.

VIDEO SCREEN

The video display device associated with your computer.

WAIT

A command file command that interrupts command file processing and waits for a single character input from the keyboard with a WAITING prompt.

WAIT TO < memory variable name >

The same as WAIT except that the TO clause causes the keyboard character to be stored in the named memory variable.

INDEX

QUIT,18,115
Quad Density,59
Query Language,120,126
Query Language Processor,124,126

READ,198
RECALL,107
RELOADING,103
RENAME,70
REPLACE,35,37
REPLACE for condition,111
REPLACE on condition,99
REPLACEMENTS,37
REPORT,43,120
REPORT FOR,124
REPORT TO PRINT,120
RETURN (command),196
RUB Key,88
Random Access,142
Re-Indexing,107,146
Read/Write Head,57
Record,6,14,15
Record Lockout,148
Record Number,14,25
Record Size (maximum),78
Record Size Indicator,24
Record Structure,20
Related,3
Relation,81
Relational,149
Relational Algebra,127
Relational Calculus,127
Relational Database,81,149
Report Form Name,43
Response Time,180
Restriction,130
Return Key,17,19
Right Justification,41,75

SAY,198